Acknowledgments

I am grateful to many people who have contributed to my life and the writing of this book.

First and foremost, I am grateful to my wife, Marie Ann, whose unwavering love, support, and belief in me kept me going even during the dark days we went through.

I am grateful to my children and grandchildren, with whom I am happy to share my success.

I am thankful to my core team, who have worked with me for over twenty years and helped me keep it real.

I acknowledge all the individuals I have encountered over the past 40-plus years—clients, candidates, and contacts—many of whom have become dear friends and have provided me with invaluable business opportunities.

Despite our ending, I thank my uncle for allowing me to learn and grow up in the business.

Finally, a special acknowledgment to my dear friend and author Anthony Celano, who encouraged me to put my story into a book and whose guidance, advice, and friendship have been invaluable

RESILIENCE:

MY FAMILY BUSINESS JOURNEY AND UNFULFILLED EXPECTATIONS

Len "Adams" Eidlen

Dedication

This book is dedicated to my family: my wife, Marie Ann, who has been my rock; my daughter, Heather; my sons, Matt and Greg; and my grandchildren, Lilly, Joseph, Michael, Nicholas, Jack, Marie, Valentina, and Lucas. They are my life and keep me motivated every day.

"The best revenge is massive success." – Frank Sinatra

This quote hangs on the wall of my office, and I believe it perfectly captures the essence of my life and career, as outlined in this book. My true story has been almost 50 years in the making. It illustrates challenges that many businesses face, especially when family is involved. At times, this story is raw and humorous, but it also demonstrates that no situation is insurmountable if one possesses a strong work ethic, belief in oneself, and the resilience to overcome challenges. I hope it provides valuable lessons to anyone who may find themselves in a difficult situation, reminding them that there is always light at the end of the tunnel.

Chapter 1

The Beginning of The End

"WE NEED TO GET RID OF YOUR DAUGHTER," my uncle Tony said to me in June 2002, beginning a chain of events that transformed my life.

My daughter, Heather, was a 20-year-old college student working for the staffing firm I ran for my uncle. She ran our temp payroll and had other administrative duties, putting in about 20 hours a week. She always performed well. Payroll was always on time, and we never had an issue with her performance.

"Why?" I asked.

"We just must," answered my uncle.

"Who will do the payroll, onboarding, and the other   administrative duties she handles for us?"

"Don't worry about it," he replied dismissively.

Since I was fully responsible for all the company's day-to-day activities, including marketing, operations, recruiting, and administration, I knew that this did not make sense. I smelled another agenda behind it.

I told him that even though Heather was my daughter, I would do what he said, only if he could demonstrate how the payroll would be done and who would handle her other duties. I needed to hear his plan.

"Just do it," he told me.

The fact was that it was not our internal payroll I was concerned about. My daughter handled the payroll for our numerous temporary staff members on assignment to various client sites. If not prepared on time, that payroll would cause a disaster for the business.

In addition, after the payroll was completed, our billing was prepared. This billing was the company's lifeblood because it brought in monthly revenue. I could not even imagine what his plan was moving forward.

Whatever plan my uncle had, he did not share it with me. We ended our meeting without a resolution. He left my office, confident I would carry out his order without further questions.

I found it odd that almost two weeks had passed without a word from him. At the time, I didn't realize why he was not around much, but those reasons became more evident weeks later.

My uncle was not in the office as we approached the summer months. However, I usually heard from him every few days or so. Silence for two weeks was unusual.

My daughter answered the phone when my uncle called the office on the Thursday before the July 4th weekend.

"What the f*ck are you still doing there?" He crudely asked.

She immediately transferred the call to me without responding to his crass comment. My uncle began a tirade about how I needed to follow his directions. I again asked him how we were going to handle the payroll and the other responsibilities she had. He told me not to be concerned. I then said to him that it was no problem, that I would do what he asked, and that he could figure out the next steps.

It should be noted that my biggest concern was making sure the business would run smoothly. The fact that he would potentially hurt the company's operation with my daughter's firing caused me great concern.

I brought my daughter into the office and shared with her what had happened. I also told her this situation was not over and that I would get to the bottom of things because something didn't smell right.

My daughter took things in stride because she knew I would get to the bottom. Since she still lived at home, she wasn't overly concerned about the financial impact of being unemployed would have on her.

I called my uncle and told him I had followed his orders and was leaving for the holiday weekend. One can only imagine the mixed feelings I had. I was angry, confused and upset. I wasn't quite sure what was behind this unusual behavior.

This exchange with my uncle marked the beginning of the end of a 45-year personal relationship and a 34-year professional relationship. Tony had always been someone I admired and respected as an uncle, a boss, and a mentor.

Before this difficulty, we had an excellent relationship. He provided me with exceptional guidance and was almost like a second father. This is why I couldn't understand what was going on. After all these years together, I couldn't grasp the change in his thought process towards me and my daughter. I knew that my daughter didn't do anything to cause him to be angry with her.

For some unknown reason, he was on a cost-cutting kick that should have begun with cutting expenses and other employees.

I could only assume that this was a personal attack to throw me off balance. What made things more baffling was that he had insinuated that I was building the business for my future for many years.

I foolishly believed that we were moving in that direction in 2002. After all, at this point, he was 86 years old. While he did have three grown children, he kept assuring me that they did not want anything to do with the business.

I had devoted 34 years of my life to my uncle and the company. In hindsight, I may have been a bit naive. This situation proved to be the beginning of a complete change in my life. For someone who prided himself on being on top of his game, this was something I didn't see coming.

I need to go back to the beginning for the reader to fully understand the dynamics of my relationship with my uncle

Chapter 2

The Beginning …..

When I was two years old, my mother passed away, and my father was left to raise me alone. Despite the challenges, he had a strong support system in his mother and sisters. Thankfully, my father's sister took me in to help raise me with her two sons; I received love and support from my Aunt Helen, Uncle Albee, and my cousins, Dennis and Lee. They became the family I knew at that young age.

After a couple of years, my father Mel needed to move past his grief and get on with his life. While he was grateful to my aunts and grandmother, he wanted to settle down again and give me a regular upbringing.

My father met the woman who would later become his wife when he took my grandmother to visit a friend in Brooklyn. Katie Francese was a former neighbor of my grandmother from when they lived on Bayard Street in Little Italy. Katie now lived with her daughter, Catherine, who had just given birth to a baby boy. Katie also had a single daughter, Angela, who was present during that visit. I suspect my grandmother had an ulterior motive for making that visit - to possibly match my widower father with her friend's single daughter.

My father and Angela hit it off immediately. After a short courtship, they married, making Angela the stepmother of a five-year-old boy. Aside from my having a new mother, I also had a new set of uncles, aunts, grandparents, and cousins.

I am sure that it was not easy for someone to marry a man with a five-year-old son. Marriage was already difficult, and this added complication made it even more so. However, Angela, whom I always referred to as my mother, not my stepmother, rose to the challenge. She raised me with my two brothers, Stephen and Mel, whom she went on to have with my father. My new mother's sister Catherine was married to Tony, the uncle who would significantly impact my life.

Growing up, we spent a great deal of time with my mother's sister, her husband, and her children.

As a young boy, being around my new mother's family, I was never considered an outsider. They embraced me as a family member.

So, as the reader can see, my future employer and I had a long relationship.

****

Tony was a knock-around guy who could easily have been confused with being a wise guy. While he did have friends in that world with whom he had grown up on the Lower East Side of Manhattan and in Red Hook, Brooklyn, he did not engage in any criminal activities. He was a completely legitimate businessman.

He respected the people he grew up with but kept them at arm's length. I know this firsthand because we had numerous conversations about how his business could have been much more substantial if he allowed contracts to be attained from people in "the underworld." He did not want to be accountable to anyone.

He was not educated in the traditional sense of the word. However, he was, in my mind, an intelligent businessman. He had a solid understanding of numbers and buiness, comparable to someone with an MBA. He possessed a keen business acumen and knew how to persuade people to do what he wanted.

As a physically imposing man with a broad chest and a booming voice, he handled himself well in business and social situations. Tony could easily connect with "street guys" and business professionals, seamlessly transitioning between the two. He was equally at ease socializing with his country club acquaintances as with his old friends from Red Hook or Mulberry Street. He was a shrewd negotiator who consistently managed to steer negotiations in his favor. He possessed street smarts that he effectively applied to business scenarios.

He was a devoted family man who cherished his wife and would do anything for his three children. They lived in a two-family home in Dyker Heights, Brooklyn. He made sure they attended the best schools and enjoyed a comfortable lifestyle. While on the exterior, he appeared gruff he was utterly soft when it came to his family.

Chapter 3

Growing Up in Knickerbocker Village

Understanding my journey by knowing how and where I grew up is crucial.

The apartment complex I was raised in was Knickerbocker Village. It was located between the Brooklyn and Manhattan bridges, two blocks from the East River on the lower east side of Manhattan.

It consisted of a square block with 12 buildings, each with 13 stories and ten apartments on every floor.

Since the 1800s, the neighborhood has been the landing point for scores of immigrants from Italy, Russia, and Ireland.

When Knickerbocker Village was built in 1934, scores of immigrants from Little Italy and other parts of the Lower East Side moved in. Most families have lived there for generations. As a result, almost every family there is related by blood or marriage; some families have known each other for generations. Knickerbocker and the surrounding blocks were like a small-town community. I had relatives in almost every one of the 12 buildings—grandparents, aunts, uncles, great-aunts, great-uncles, and cousins.

The neighborhood was home to a diverse mix of careers, including judges, lawyers, doctors, business owners, longshoremen, fishmongers, printers, and truck drivers for the

Journal American newspaper, civil servants, and Wall Street back-office staff. Others would spend their days at the various "social clubs" located throughout the neighborhood.

To survive in such a tough area, one needed "street smarts." Friends had to be chosen wisely; otherwise, getting into trouble or being on the wrong side of the law was easy.

Knickerbocker Village has also served as the backdrop for many books and movies set in the mob genre. Thanks to the various social clubs, it was a safe neighborhood. By the time I was in my teens, however, a change was happening. Drugs were starting to infiltrate the neighborhood, as they did in most neighborhoods in the late '60s and early '70s.

I am not denigrating the neighborhood's makeup. On the contrary, I would not have traded growing up there for anywhere else. It was a very family-oriented area, with salt-of-the-earth residents of all nationalities and careers.

Fortunately, my parents instilled a deep sense of right and wrong in my brothers and me. They ensured my time was filled with positive social activities to keep me off the streets. I was a Boy Scout and a CYO member, and I even played guitar in a band.

In 1969, I was a freshman at LaSalle Academy, a small Catholic high school in Manhattan. We weren't poor, but we weren't rich either. My father worked for his parents' Private Sanitation business, Bayard Carting, for several years.

My grandparents had taken over the business from my great-grandfather on my grandmother's side and operated it for many years.

My grandfather had recently sold the family's business. Unfortunately, this did not net my father any financial gain; He had to start a career over again, returning to the Customs House broker he had left years earlier to join the family business. At 44, he was re-starting his career with the pressure of a wife, three kids, and Catholic school tuition, and the cost of a vacation home in Greenwood Lake that we shared with my two aunts. Since he had taken a much lower salary than he earned at his parents' company, he had a great deal on his plate.

We always lived well, food was always on the table, and we enjoyed our summers and weekends at the lake house. My father never complained and ensured we were cared for and had everything we wanted and needed.

****

Shortly after starting high school, one of my cousins started a part-time job as a messenger at a large law firm. When he told me they were looking to hire additional part-time students, I jumped at the chance to earn some pocket money. This job would keep me occupied and out of trouble. I started the part-time job at the beginning of my freshman year.

Although this was against my father's wishes, I took on the job to make extra money and not depend on my parents for additional expenses. Although I knew my parents would never turn down my requests, I saw this as an opportunity to be responsible.

The law firm was an old-school, prestigious white-shoe firm. My cousin and I would go there after school and spend several hours in the mail room. We would deliver mail and documents to the lawyers in the office and clients around the city. The job introduced me to a grown-up world, allowing me to interact with lawyers, office managers, and secretaries. Inasmuch as I loved the firm, I had difficulty handling any deliveries that entailed taking a subway.

The root of this was a fear instilled in me by my father. For as long as I can remember, my father used to tell me not to take the subway.

"They are dangerous," he would tell me.

"Wherever you have to go, if you can't walk, take a bus or a cab, I will drive you."

This came from a place of being protective towards my brothers and me. I never viewed it as a negative. It just shaped who I was. Even though I lived in Manhattan, I carried this fear my entire life. While sometimes I couldn't avoid taking the subway, I did my best to avoid it. However, my lack of experience left me with limited knowledge of how to navigate the NYC subway system. This shortcoming caused me to leave this job after several months. I was not cut out to be a messenger. I did not possess an essential skill necessary for that job...... the ability to travel by subway! Later in my adult years, I did learn how to use the subway system, but I would do so as a last resort. That irrational fear resurfaced after 9/11. As of the writing of this book, I have not been on a subway since 2001.

Chapter 4

A Life-Changing Decision

Whenever I tell someone what I do for a living, I am always asked how I started in the recruiting industry. In the late 1960s and early 1970s, most people did not consider the recruiting industry a career option.

The short answer is because of a snowstorm.

A snowstorm?

A severe snowstorm in 1969 crippled NYC, causing businesses to close. The city came to a standstill.

My uncle Tony called my mom after the snowstorm and asked if I would like to come to work part-time at his employment agency. He knew I had recently left the part-time messenger job. He reasoned that since I lived on the Lower East Side and was only a 15-minute walk to the office on Broadway and John Street, he could give me the keys to the office. This way, I could get to the office in case of another snowstorm or similar emergency. Mind you, this is before voicemail, cell phones, etc. He always wanted to ensure someone was available to answer a phone call.

I knew nothing about the business. I didn't even know what an "employment agency "was. All I knew was he would pay me $1.50 an hour in cash to come to the office after school. I would help with filing, answering phones, etc. I eagerly seized the opportunity to have to no longer navigate the NYC subway system.

So here I was, a 15-year-old teenager who was an average student, spending my afternoons in an office. In comparison, my friends were out playing basketball. I was earning some pocket money.

The office was in a run-down building at 180 Broadway in Manhattan's financial district. In commercial real estate, office buildings are typically classified as A, B, or C; the building we were in may have been classified as a D class. A women's dress store was on the first floor, and a Jewish deli was attached. The office was not as prestigious as the law firm at One Wall Street where I was previously. That was class-A building that also housed the Irving Trust Company headquarters

Several years earlier, my uncle had taken over the firm Kling Personnel (KPA) from the original owner, Sidney Kling. The company was relatively small, with roughly 6-7 employees. The office consisted of an open area with about eight desks and a small private office for my uncle, the boss. The employees were all at least 10-15 years older than I was.

The business's primary activity consisted of recruiters calling various companies in the downtown area to provide employees for their open jobs. The primary roles were in Wall Street Brokerage, Insurance, and Steamship companies. Applicants would answer advertisements, or the recruiters would reach out to those applicants who had previously applied for a position.

The firm had an office manager, Richard Ullo, who went by the name Richard York. Richard was a sharply dressed guy who was an excellent producer and manager. He ran the desk that provided staff to the Wall Street Brokerage industry and was also my uncle's right-hand man.

He was personable and had a good following of clients and candidates. We worked side by side for almost nine years until he had a falling out with my uncle. More about that later.

Richard was an exemplary employee who did his best to keep the lively cast of characters under control. He was very good at his job, and I learned a great deal by listening to how he handled things.

One of the things he taught me was not to emulate his style but to develop my own. It was great advice that served me well.

The jobs they handled were Wall Street brokerage back-office clerks, receptionists, secretaries, typists, etc. The demand for those individuals was high, so there was a consistent flow of candidates and jobs. The waiting room was always full of candidates applying for the advertised jobs.

As a 15-year-old, I felt like I was in a grown-up playground. With the colorful mix of people in our open area, there was nonstop banter and lightheartedness. Despite the joking and laughing, the environment was very conducive to success. Candidates often returned to visit, bringing their friends, and thus sent constant referrals.

My job was to do anything I was asked. I would file, sweep floors, type invoices, and even deliver resumes - all downtown, no subways. I used to accompany my uncle when he went to Goldsmith Brothers to buy office supplies. On those occasions, we would have lengthy talks about the business, and he would offer tidbits of life advice. He always told me, "Don't let your right hand know what your left hand is doing." I never entirely understood what he meant by that until years later.

I stayed there throughout high school, taking on additional responsibilities as the opportunity presented itself. Part of those responsibilities consisted of typing and sending the bills to clients. The business was very active; I saw numerous weekly invoices mailed to clients. The amounts weren't large, but there was volume. To someone my age, sending 20 invoices to companies for $300-500 each week seemed like a good business. Those amounts were based on a small percentage of the applicant's salary that the client was charged. Therefore, if a company hired a receptionist for $10400 per year, we would bill that company 5% of the annual salary as a one-time fee ($520.) This was a relatively new concept. Prior to 1970, the job applicant would pay a fee to obtain a job. A change occurred in the industry,

29

the first of several to happen after 1970. The industry went from charging the applicant a fee to charging the client a fee that was capped at 5% of salary, later raised to 10%. The most significant change occurred a couple of years later. Agency fees were no longer capped at 10% and were open to negotiation. The industry was in the throes of change, and I was there right at the beginning. Little did I know what the future would hold. It was the start of the industry becoming much more professional and profitable.

Little by little, I became more and more enamored with the business. After graduating high school in 1972, I started college at Pace College, now known as Pace University. I used to plan my schedule around being able to go back to the office between classes. I knew I wanted to be more involved in the business.

Chapter 5

Pivotal Moments

There have been several pivotal moments in my life that all seemed to happen simultaneously.

First, I was losing interest and not focusing on my classes, which caused my grades to suffer. I believed a real-world environment would be a better education for me. This, coupled with the fact that we were taking out loans to pay for the school, made me very uncomfortable as if I were throwing out money and mortgaging my future.

The final and most significant turning point was when I began dating my now-wife. We met at the beginning of my second semester of college. I knew right away that this would be the person I would spend my life with. In January of 1973, I went on a blind date. The circumstances of the date were interesting. My friend John Isoldi planned to take his girlfriend out to celebrate his birthday. Since he attended college in California and was home for the holidays, this was his last weekend to celebrate. The only wrinkle for him was that his girlfriend was spending the weekend with her best friend, Marie Ann. She wanted to cancel their plans since she did not want to leave her friend. John's idea was to have me go along with them to celebrate his birthday.

I had a few issues with his plan. First, I didn't have any money. Second, I didn't want to date a girl from the neighborhood. I didn't know her, so it had nothing to do with her. It was only because I felt it would be uncomfortable if we did not hit it off. Additionally, I was not interested in getting involved with anyone. I wanted to focus on school. The third issue was I had exams that week and was planning on studying. John was very persuasive in convincing me to change my mind so that he would not have to change his plans. He promised that he would loan me the money. After all, we were only going to the movies and out for a drink. As for dating a neighborhood girl, he suggested that I only needed to go out with her this one time—no need to get involved. As for studying, he reminded me I had all day on Sunday. The clincher, however, was that he threatened to beat the crap out of me if I didn't grant him this favor. Enough said ...I agreed to go on the date. That decision turned out to be not only a turning point in my life but probably one of the best decisions in my life.

The inexpensive movie was not just a movie—drinks and food followed at Hawaii Kai, an expensive tourist nightclub in Times Square. Transportation consisted of cabs back and forth .... not an inexpensive night. Regarding not getting involved with someone from the neighborhood, that idea went out the window when I met Marie Ann. As far as studying Accounting on Sunday was concerned, I decided, instead, to double-date again with John, his girlfriend, and Marie Ann.

I did not fail my accounting exam the following Monday. However, the grade I received did not do much for my GPA. I enrolled at Pace with a plan to become a CPA. My grasp of accounting principles and lack of interest derailed that plan.

I was not living up to my potential as far as my grades were concerned. I still recall my accounting professor's assignment in my second accounting semester. The assignment was to reconcile a set of books. Before computers, we used sizeable green journal paper. I examined this set of books for hours and hours but could not reconcile. I was off by five cents. Five cents! I finally became utterly frustrated. I handed the assignment in the next day with a nickel taped to the paper. The professor sternly asked me what I thought I was doing with the nickel taped to the page. I confidently told him my time would be worth more than the nickel if I were a business owner. If I were out of reconciliation by that amount, I would just put the nickel back in the business or write it off. The professor looked at me and laughed.

"You will never be an accountant, but you will probably be a good businessman."

I took the compliment along with the "D" for the assignment.

An experience in an English class cemented my decision not to continue attending school full-time. We were tasked with reading a book and writing a comparison to another book. I did not read either book, opting to skim through the cliff notes. I turned in what I thought was a beautifully written paper. When I received my grade, the professor gave me a D plus with a note to see him after class. I asked him why I received a D plus. He told me when he read my paper, he quickly realized I did not know what I was writing about. However, I did such a beautiful job of bullshitting my way through; he didn't have the heart to fail me.

"You will probably be in sales at some point in your career," he told me.

These experiences were part of the beginning of my figuring out my strengths and weaknesses. However, I realized that I was not putting the effort into school that I should have.

I decided that school would have to take a back seat. My parents tried to discourage me but to no avail. As my father used to tell me, I had a thick head!

Although I knew I was disappointing my parents, I reassured them that I would return in the future. I'm unsure if I believed it or if they did, but it was a way to soften the blow. I felt confident I was making the right decision for myself at that moment in time. A large part of my drive to succeed throughout my life was to prove to my parents that I was not a failure. Looking back, I had a positive outcome. I might have thought differently if I were faced with those decisions again. Then again, I may have done it the same way. It's a challenging situation to reflect on.

Chapter 6

My Great Plan

At 19 years old, I thought I had a great plan: I was dropping out of school and asking my uncle to hire me full-time. When I approached him, he was not enthusiastic about the idea. He told me he didn't think I had what it took to be successful in the business. Challenge accepted! I asked him to give me a few months to prove myself. I had already spent four years listening and observing, so I had a good idea of how to handle myself. I needed to figure out how to be a recruiter/account manager.

I started working full-time in the business the summer after my freshman year. I was paid an hourly rate, which did not amount to much, but I was anxious to get started in the industry.

One of my cousins had a good friend whose cousin was the Hiring Manager for the buying office of a chain of men's clothing stores. This is an excellent example of the six degrees of separation theory. When I met the Hiring Manager, she seemed to like me, especially since I was connected to her through only two degrees of separation. She mentioned that she needed high school graduates who could pass a simple 10-question math test. If they could pass, they would be hired.

She asked if I could help her. True to my usual way of doing things, I agreed to assist her. This was going to be easy, so I took the job order and started the process of filling the jobs.

I began calling through my social circle and found people who would jump at the chance. Several friends had dropped out of college and needed to find a job. They would be my first source.

I placed my first one. The client then told me they needed a second one. She explained that she could hire as many as 5-10 + a week. The salaries were $105-115 per week, and we charged a fee of $275-315 Per person. I put all my energy into this account. I found candidates, screened them, ensured they could pass a simple math test, and sold them on this opportunity. We started placing 10-15 per week.: that's the good news. The bad news is that 30% of them would quit after a week or two. So, there was a constant turnover of candidates. The client was ok with that. They had an expectation that employees would not stay at that level of position. I was generating business and keeping an applicant flow going. I was a superstar in my mind.! I enjoyed the challenge. I felt I was helping a client and the candidates getting the jobs. This gave me an excellent introduction to what the business entailed.

I quickly realized that if this company hired candidates such as those, their competitors probably had the exact needs. So, I tried to expand my activities by contacting other retail buying offices in NY, but my attempt was unsuccessful. One issue was that this account was my only success story. I only opened the account because of a personal relationship. I didn't know how to cold sell to open an account. Another problem was that our firm was perceived as a Wall Street recruiting firm due to our location and reputation. This was more of an issue then, unlike today.

After several months of rejection, I recognized that breaking into the retail/garment industry would not happen. I continued servicing my one client until they hit a dry spell. At that point, I felt like I was in trouble. It seemed like my plan to become a recruiter was falling apart.

Not one to take failure easily, I decided I needed a plan B. I surveyed the office and noticed that there were two people working on Transportation/import Export, two on Wall Street, and two on Insurance. In hindsight, I'm unsure why I didn't try to join any of those departments, which were known as "desks". Perhaps my ego drove me to prove I could build something from scratch. What stood out to me was the absence of anyone supplying staff to the banking industry.

I told my uncle that I wanted to build a banking department/desk. He gave me the green light to go ahead. I think he recognized my determination and knew I had something to prove.

In hindsight, I didn't have any contacts or educational connections. All I had was sheer determination and grit.

When asked why he robbed banks, Willie Sutton famously said, "That's where the money is."

Similarly, I chose to service the banking industry because it's a people-intensive field that requires hiring many employees, and I wanted to fulfill that need.

Chapter 7

Early 1970's -My Alter Ego

In 1974, I started developing a banking recruiting desk. One of the things I needed to do was develop a "desk name." A desk name was the name a recruiter would use when calling on companies and candidates. There was nothing nefarious about using a different name. It was done primarily to simplify the process of leaving messages. Also, in the very early years of the recruiting industry, there was a great deal of bias regarding various ethnicities. Using a desk name allowed the recruiter to mask their ethnicity and thus avoid any potential bias against them by

45

corporate America. By the time I started, while the bias was beginning to ebb, the practice of a desk name continued.

Almost every competitor I was up against in those days used a "desk name." My competitors had last names like, Salem, Bogart, Carter, Tucker, etc. none of these were their real names. I was in good company in continuing the practice.

I decided to use the "desk name" of Len Adams.

I chose the name Len Adams for several reasons.

It was easy to say, easy to remember, and had a waspish sound. I called on companies that traditionally did not like ethnic-sounding names. Second, an easy-to-say and spell name is much easier when cold calling on the phone and leaving a message. It is memorable and makes leaving messages easier. It is essential to realize this is the early 70s before woke, dei, and all the societal advancements of today.

Adams was always at the beginning of any list of memberships, conference attendees, etc. I started using that name, and it became my alter ego. The real me was still somewhat introverted and shy. As Len Adams, I became more confident and outgoing. I'd bet a psychologist could have had a field day with me!

Having more balls than brains, I embarked on my plan. Despite feeling dejected, I was determined to make inroads within the banking industry. I began using The EZ Directory of Banks and Brokers, which listed every bank in NYC.

I began calling all the banks' CEO's office in the directory. The CEO's Executive Assistant would generally answer the phone. I would politely ask to speak with the CEO. The EA, doing her job, would always ask who was calling and the reason for the call. I would introduce myself and explain that my company offered recruiting services to banks. I explained that I wanted to discuss their hiring challenges with the CEO. Surprisingly, no one hung up.

In almost all cases, the EA would tell me kindly that I needed to speak with the Personnel Department, now known as Human Resources, about those matters. I always asked if they could provide me with the name and number of the contact I needed to speak with. Almost 10 out of 10 times, they would give it to me. Sometimes, they would even transfer the call. If not, I would call the Personnel contact and explain that the CEO's office told me to speak with them. I positioned it in such a way it seemed as though I was referred to them directly by the CEO. They weren't sure if I was a relative, a friend, or a business contact of the CEO, but they would almost always listen to my pitch., especially with the Waspish name of Len Adams.

I cannot claim a 100% success rate, but I successfully initiated relationships with the Personnel Department to stay connected with them. By establishing rapport, I eventually received orders from them.

After making these calls for some time, I realized I needed to define my target market further. Some banks were unresponsive, so I categorized them as a C list. Some showed some interest, so I put them on my B list. Finally, some were very receptive. Those were the ones I would closely follow up with. I also noticed a shift in the banking market. Banks from foreign countries and out-of-state were opening offices in NY. When I called those institutions, they were the most receptive. Especially since only a few recruiters were reaching out to them. I decided to focus my attention on those institutions. I developed an alphabetic list of bank contacts I would call them religiously every week.

The bank names that started with A, B, and C were called on Monday, D, E, F, Tuesday, etc. until I got to Friday. My style was very easygoing and not pushy. I would make small talk, tell them a joke, and ask them to keep me in mind if I could help them with any open jobs. I broke every sales rule in the book. The rules said you must try to sell them on a candidate or push hard for a job. I decided that wasn't my personality. I seemed to be making progress! I started to receive orders and filled them as quickly as I received them. A significant turning point was when I reversed my call sequence one week. I started calling the banks at the end of the alphabet on Monday and gradually making my way to the beginning of the alphabet by the end of the week. To my surprise, on Friday, when I reached out to the people, I usually call on Monday, they asked me why they hadn't heard from me Monday. This indicated that I was making a positive impact and gaining recognition. I was gradually building the beginning of a strong banking desk for the firm.

As I continued the building process, I came to several conclusions. First, I needed an education to compete in the business world. Second, I needed to completely immerse myself in recruiting for the banking industry. I knew I needed to be visible and vocal. Despite the issues I had with my uncle later in life, they do not negate the many positive things he did for me early in my career. He knew I was introverted, so he had me attend Dale Carnegie to improve my public speaking skills. I was an introverted person who had great difficulty speaking in public. Thanks to the Dale Carnegie course, my public speaking abilities improved significantly. As a result, my confidence improved, and I was empowered to take on numerous public speaking activities throughout my career, including teaching seminars on Personnel Consulting at Wagner College and Business Ethics at St John's University. In addition, I have engaged in a myriad of presentations and seminars for professional associations and delivered lectures on various topics in later years. These were activities I would never have imagined myself doing.

Once I completed Dale Carnegie, I suggested that he allow me to enroll in classes at the American Institute of Banking (AIB). I thought that by attending AIB, I would learn banking terminology and practices. Also, I would be able to make contacts that I could use to develop as candidates and potential clients. Those AIB credits would also be transferrable towards my degree at Pace when I reconvene my college courses.

The classes taught me specific details about the various jobs of the people I was placing. I did well in class. In fact, in one class on International Operations, I scored the highest grade and was the only non-banker. One year after completing the course, I placed my teacher in a new position. The fee we earned more than paid for the tuition.

After completing AIB, my uncle agreed to have me register for school at night to complete my degree. He did this because he saw something in me that he could cultivate.

In the early 1970s, our professional association introduced a professional designation known as CEC — Certified Employment Consultant, later changed to CPC — Certified Personnel Consultant. This initiative aimed to elevate the professionalism of our industry. To obtain the certification, individuals were required to have two years of experience in the recruiting industry. There was also a requirement to complete a series of courses and pass a four-hour exam on personnel practices, laws, and regulations. At 21, my uncle encouraged me to take the course and sit for the exam. Because, at that time, there weren't too many 21-year-olds who had already completed two years in the industry, I became one of the youngest candidates to attain the certification. This designation aligned with my feeling that I was involved in a profession, not just a job. It furthered my desire to help professionalize the business.

Uncle Tony allowed me to re-enroll at Pace at night to complete my business degree. So, I started attending Pace University at night, working during the day, and immersing myself in the business world.

In October of 1974, I proposed to my girlfriend. In June 1976, at the ages of 22 and 21, we married in the beautiful old parish of St. Joseph on Monroe Street, across from Knickerbocker Village. Despite not having much money and possibly not being fully prepared for marriage, we were determined to start our life together. We rented a one-bedroom apartment in Knickerbocker Village. Despite the challenges, we were in love and felt confident about building our lives together. We knew we would be able to create a good life together. As of the writing of this book (2024), we have been married for 48 years, together for 51, and have produced three children and eight grandchildren. My wife has been my rock and my partner. I was fortunate to gain in-laws, Mary and Joe Cicero, who treated me like a son. I was never able to make a mother-in-law joke because there was not a thing I could complain about.

As a married man, I was more determined than ever to become successful. Every day, I made calls to develop business, service the business I brought in, and attend school at night. Then, in 1978, another pivot happened. Richard, the office manager I mentioned at the beginning of the book, argued with my uncle. My uncle had made promises to him that he was not fulfilling. They had a falling out. This falling out led Richard to leave the company to start his own recruiting firm.

I was producing close to Richards's numbers. In retrospect, I believe my uncle may have felt he didn't need Richard anymore. He may have feared that Richard and I would form an alliance and put my uncle in a position of weakness. In hindsight, he may have been right. Even though that thought never crossed my mind, I was completely loyal to my boss.

The day Richard left, he told me,

"Watch your back; your uncle Tony will promise you the world and never make good on his promises."

I was insulted and told Richard that he was out of line speaking about my family in that manner. As a result, Richard and I didn't speak for over twenty years. More on this later. He did go on to build a very successful recruiting business. I was now tasked with being the "go-to" guy for the office. I became the "heir apparent, "as I was referred to by the staff.

At 24 years old, I was now primarily responsible for managing all office activities and continuing to generate revenue. I was moving at 100 miles an hour. I loved every minute of it. I would start my day at 8 AM and spend the day calling client prospects and interviewing candidates. Three nights a week and some Saturdays, I would go to class at Pace. On my off nights, I would do my homework. I would also make calls at night to reach candidates I couldn't contact during the day. I had quite a full schedule. I was still not making big money with all this responsibility. My uncle told me that the money would come if I built the business. I accepted that because I was young, naïve, and focused on creating the desk and keeping things moving. I don't know how my wife put up with it because there was always "more month than money." I rationalized it to myself and my wife that good things would come eventually. I would be the best I could be in business and become successful or die trying. Fortunately, my wife was and is excellent at budgeting. She knew how to stretch our money to make ends meet. In addition, we did not live an extravagant lifestyle.

Chapter 8

Building, Learning, Building

I kept establishing and servicing new accounts as the late 1970s and early 1980s unfolded. We started hiring assistants to help me with the recruiting. I managed the office, trained the staff, and did everything necessary to keep the business going.

I made it a point to learn and continuously try new things to improve. For example, one of our account managers had a relationship with a high school in Queens. He ran a program where he would visit the school and speak to the graduating seniors about how to fill out job applications, provide interview tips, and discuss the job market. Since we handled many clerical and secretarial jobs at the time, and this high school had very few college-bound students, it was a great candidate source and provided great public relations for the firm.

I thought, if we had one interested school, why not approach others? So, I embarked on an initiative to offer these free job search seminars to other high schools in Brooklyn, Queens, Staten Island, and NYC. At one point, I presented this program at 10 to 12 high schools annually from April to May. We collected and processed applications for graduating students seeking secretarial positions. We successfully placed many of them. This provided us with a good following and a great referral base. I also struck a deal with one of our large commercial bank clients. We agreed that we would give them a certain number of students for free as an incentive to provide us with other positions. We did this for several years until we found our business pivoting away from those types of jobs. Also, many of the schools we had relationships with started to transition from commercial and secretarial programs and more towards college preparatory programs.

Recognizing this evolution in the market, I developed a plan to change the scope of the business. Given what was happening in the market, I aimed to create a three-pronged approach to the business...

1 Expand to provide executive search, Mid-level and staff recruiting, as well as temporary services

2 Hire a more professional staff and cut down on turnover,

3 Continue to build areas of industry specialists.

To accomplish this, I needed to start with me.

I began diligently reading the American Banker and other industry publications. I attended any banking industry functions I could access., I was moving at full speed and wouldn't slow down.

One morning in 1976, while perusing the American Banker, I read about a consortium of banks from the US and the Middle East that were planning to establish a brand-new joint venture in New York.

I realized that if this were a new venture, they would need to hire many people at all levels.   I began researching the consortium participants. After making numerous phone calls, I was able to identify who the newly named CEO would be. Before the internet and computers, one had to be somewhat of a detective to find this information out. It also wasn't easy to always get information from people, but I was relentless.

Armed with this information, I mailed the newly named CEO a letter to introduce myself and to arrange a meeting. Much to my surprise, I received a call from him, inviting me to meet him. I was both elated and nervous since it was potentially a big deal to be able to staff a start-up bank. I arranged to meet him at his temporary office in the basement of the Bankers Trust building near Liberty Street. Bankers Trust was one of the consortium banks involved in the entity. I met with the CEO, a white-haired gentleman in his 60s. He was very waspish and proper. I was a 22-year-old kid putting myself in front of the CEO of a large, very politically connected institution being organized.

During our 90-minute meeting, the CEO, whose first name was Kevin, asked me about my thoughts on recruitment for the company, my stance on discrimination, and various other topics. I remained composed and tried not to let his intimidating demeanor affect me. As the meeting ended, he shook my hand, thanked me for coming in, and said,

"We will be in touch."

I walked out of that meeting telling myself,

"There is no way in hell I am getting this account."

About a month later, I received a call from Al Schrang. Al identified himself as the Chief Operating Officer of the newly formed entity. He invited me to meet him at the site of their new offices. I didn't know what to expect, but I happily accepted the invitation to the meeting.

I went to the office at 345 Park Avenue to meet with Mr. Schrang. The offices were still under construction. I found him in the middle of a construction site, with a desk in a cleared-out area. When I walked in, he told me Kevin was impressed with my openness and honesty and suggested we meet to discuss their recruiting needs. He showed me the organizational chart of all the positions that needed to be filled and asked me where I could assist. I reviewed the chart with him and gave him my opinion on salaries, time to fill, the candidates I thought I could find, and so on.

"Great," he told me.

" I believe Kevin was right. You can be of assistance to us."

I was thrilled to be getting the contract. However, I had a potential problem on my mind.

"Mr. Schrang, I am very grateful to be given this opportunity and look forward to being a good resource to the bank. However, I must tell you that I am getting married in three weeks and will be on my honeymoon for a week. If necessary, I will postpone my honeymoon to get everything done for you."

HE NEARLY FELL OFF HIS CHAIR LAUGHING.

"Postpone your honeymoon?

"Are you crazy? This will be a several-month process. We can wait for you to return!".

Looking back, I can't believe I made that offer. I'm sure the wedding wouldn't have happened had I told my fiancé we weren't going on a honeymoon!

I was also quite naive about how much effort this would involve. Al Schrang and I connected at that moment. He appreciated my commitment and honesty. We built a very close relationship. I filled many positions for him, and we remained friends for many years until his passing. My firm made a great deal of money from that relationship. I didn't see anything beyond my salary, but I was building a reputation.

This was the first of numerous banks that I was able to assist with establishing operations in NYC.

Chapter 9

Exploring a New Path?

As I started my married life, money was always tight. While I appreciated my uncle paying for my night classes, I struggled to make ends meet. Despite my wife's support, she was understandably frustrated with our limited income and the long hours I was putting in. She had a job, but her salary was earmarked to help us save for a house.

We knew we would eventually start a family, and she would no longer be employed. Although we didn't argue, she did express concerns about my career and our financial future.

My wife convinced me that I should consider another career option. My brother-in-law, who was my wife's sister's husband, held a senior position at a subsidiary of Manufacturers Hanover Bank. At my wife's request, our brother-in-law helped set up an interview for me with the bank's personnel department.

I reluctantly went to the interview, partly to please my wife and partly to explore other opportunities. I dressed in my finest attire and met with the HR team, took an assessment test, and completed the interview process. To my surprise, I was offered the job at the end of the interview. I was offered a salary slightly more than I was earning

"We think you would be great in our collections department, given your experience with making phone calls,"

I asked what my duties would be. They explained that I would be responsible for calling bank customers who were delinquent in their auto or personal loan payments.

When I returned home and told my wife, she was more excited than I was. She wanted me to take the job. She told me I could count on our brother-in-law to pull some strings to eventually move me up through the organization. I was not so excited about the specific job duties. I feared that I would be calling half the people in my neighborhood who were probably late on their loan payments. Reluctantly, to satisfy my wife, I accepted the position.

The next day, I went to the office to tell Tony I was considering a new job at a bank. I must admit we had an excellent conversation. He asked me all the details and my long-range plan with the bank. I explained what the job was and my offer.

I also explained that my brother-in-law would watch out for me at the bank and eventually pull some strings to get me on a faster track. He then asked me two questions, which started me thinking. The first question was,

"What happens if your brother-in-law leaves the bank?"

The second question was

"Did I feel confident that I could move up in the bank on my own?

I honestly didn't have a concrete answer for either question. I also had some self-doubt about moving up in a large financial institution, especially without an education.

He told me that I could do what I wanted and that he would not be angry. He suggested that whatever I did, I should ensure I could count on myself to move up and not rely on someone else. Looking back, it was sound advice. Ultimately, I decided to turn down the position for several reasons. First, I didn't want to rely on someone else to advance my career. Second, not having my degree, I lacked self-esteem and was unsure if I was cut out for a position in a large corporation. Lastly, I wasn't excited about the idea of making collection calls. I explained my decision to my wife, and while she wasn't happy about it, she understood my concerns. As for my job with my uncle, I told him I was staying.

We never discussed it again. His advice seemed genuine and sincere at that moment, and I believed he had a long-term plan.

Chapter 10

Continued Growth

In the early 1980s, my life underwent significant changes. The decade brought moments of joy, growth, and sorrow. In 1981, my daughter Heather was born. Yes, it was the same daughter I had to let go of 21 years later. I also received my degree in Business from Pace with honors. This achievement further fueled my motivation to succeed. 1985 marked the birth of my son Matthew, and in 1989, my son Greg was born. So, the 80s became a time of family and professional growth for my wife and me. However, it also came with personal challenges. In 1984, my father was diagnosed with colon cancer. This news was shocking, but it wasn't entirely surprising, considering my grandfather had battled colon cancer 25 years earlier. At the time, we hadn't thought about familial risk, but in hindsight, there seemed to be a high incidence of cancer in my family. My father, within a year, had a recurrence of the cancer. This was devastating to our family. The doctors told us to get his affairs in order.

My father never gave up, nor did we let him. He underwent additional surgery, chemo, and radiation without ever getting depressed. He would have his treatments in the morning and then take the bus to his job. His positive attitude and perseverance taught me a great deal. This was when he was in his early 60s, and he continued to battle additional cancers into his

70s. He never lost hope. He lived to the age of 90 and did not pass away from cancer. This lesson stuck with me my entire life. On a side note, witnessing how he handled his cancer enabled me to get through my own colon cancer diagnosis in 2022. I am happy to report that, as of this writing, I am cancer-free.

After the birth of our daughter, we realized that our one-bedroom apartment in Knickerbocker Village was becoming too small for our family. We didn't want to raise our daughter in Manhattan, so we searched for a home in Staten Island, where my wife's siblings lived.

We searched for a house for two years, constantly chasing the prices. Everything we liked was too expensive. Even though the business was doing well, I still needed help to buy a starter home. I had numerous discussions with Tony about this, and he promised to help make it possible for us to move. In 1983, mortgage interest rates were incredibly high. This was advantageous to us since home prices started to stabilize.

One weekend, while visiting my sister-in-law in Staten Island, we were told about a house two blocks away from her. It was a ranch that was a little above what we wanted to pay. We made an offer, and it was accepted. The seller needed us to wait eight months for his new house to be ready. It was not an issue since we were in an apartment without a fixed lease. I met with my uncle to advise him that we found something. I also told him that I needed to be able to earn more money. I also needed a car since we didn't have one. He told me not to worry; I would have what I needed by the time we were ready to close on the house. Armed with this optimism, we moved ahead with the deal. I continued to produce revenue. As we came near the time to close on the house, I went to my uncle to see how I would afford the house and a car.

In terms of compensation, my uncle gave me a slight raise in my salary, but I needed more to cover my increased expenses. He also mentioned that he would provide me with a car. The car he offered was his son's 5-year-old car that was recently repaired from an accident. He told me he would give me the car, but if I ever sold it, the money would return to him. I accepted his offer because I couldn't afford to buy or lease a car. When we closed on the house, we emptied our bank account and were left without any financial cushion.

I was still confident I would keep producing and earning money. Driving to our new house, we noticed the car my uncle provided me was making a funny noise. I called my uncle, who told me to find a mechanic in Staten Island.

I brought the car to the mechanic I was referred to, who lived in my new neighborhood. He called me the next day and said the car needed brakes and a tune-up that would cost $300. It may as well have been 3 million dollars. I didn't have the $300. I called my uncle and asked him what happened. He had told me that he had the car fixed up for me. After hemming and hawing and double-talking me, he told me to do what I had to do to fix it. It was my problem. Besides, where was I going to get a car for $300? So, I borrowed the money from my father-in-law and had the car fixed.

I accepted it because, as he said, where could I get a car for $300? Blind loyalty!

My desire and motivation to be successful influenced my habits. I would consistently arrive at the office by 8 am to search for leads in the daily periodicals. I would review resumes from the mail since this was before fax and email. Candidates would mail in their resumes, call us, or walk in to apply for the jobs we advertised. It was always hectic. I would spend much of the day making calls to prospect for new clients. In between, I would review resumes, call candidates, and schedule interviews. My day didn't end at 5 pm. I would usually get home at a reasonable time unless there was a networking event, bank opening, or Professional Association meeting to attend.

However, just because I was home didn't mean my workday stopped; I would get home by 6:30 pm, eat dinner, and play with my kids for a while. At 8 pm, I would begin my calls to pitch jobs to candidates or confirm interviews. This was my routine. My wife was very patient with me as she put up with this schedule throughout our life. During the years I was with KPA, it didn't add any extra money to our pockets. However, I convinced myself I was building a reputation that would pay off one day. Also, I felt I was providing a service to the candidates and clients and justifying my salary; I don't regret working as hard as I did because it instilled in me a work ethic that ultimately helped me succeed. When I reflect on those times, I am grateful that my wife was understanding and not the jealous type. I always carried pieces of paper in my pocket with the phone numbers of people I needed to call. Another woman might have been suspicious, but my wife knew me better.

My routine also included preparing for the coming week on a Sunday night. The New York Times Help Wanted section was the recruiter's bible. I would review it to see what the competition was doing. I would look for our ads to ensure that they were correct. I would also look for companies that were advertising open positions. Since most people were home on a Sunday night, it was an optimal time to call candidates to confirm interviews for the coming week. In those days, people answered their phones! My wife was patient because I was steadfast in my commitment to do this. If we had a wedding or party to attend on a Sunday, I would routinely take a pocket full of quarters with me to make calls in between courses. Admittedly, I wouldn't make as many calls as when we were home, but there was always someone I needed to reach. My wife thought I was a little crazy. She always asked me why I worked so hard when it wasn't adding to our bank account. My response was that I still needed to justify my salary and provide the clients with the service I promised. I truly believed I would reap the rewards by building the business for my uncle.

In the summer of 1977, NYC experienced a massive blackout. That did not deter me, however. As we sat in the dark that evening, I grabbed a flashlight and went to the phone to make some calls. My wife asked me what I was doing. I explained that I had interviews scheduled for the next day and wanted to confirm them.

"But we are in a blackout," she said.

"I know," I replied. "But I am sure the lights will be on tomorrow, and business will go on as usual."

"I married a madman."

She may have been correct, but I felt compelled to act according to my diligence without hesitation.

****

After my success with the foreign bank consortium, I noticed another pattern. Foreign banks started opening in New York almost every month. The US, and particularly New York, was a sought-after location for banks from Europe, Latin America, Asia, and the Middle East to operate. They primarily focused on financing foreign trade, trading foreign currencies, and servicing the needs of US businesses headquartered in their home countries.

I had already assisted several foreign banks with establishing operations in New York. Due to my successful track record, I gained the reputation of being a start-up specialist. As more banks from the same country arrived in New York, I began receiving referrals from one bank to another from within that country.

In two separate instances, I experienced both success and failure within one month. I heard about the opening of two prominent institutions in New York City: a notable French institution and a major German institution. After conducting my research, I identified the senior people at these institutions. The French institution seemed receptive, and they referred me to their newly hired head of HR. I presented our services to her, and she agreed to meet with me. However, she ultimately chose not to utilize my services for reasons I could not ascertain. Undeterred by this setback, I pursued the German bank. Using the same approach, I was referred to the Head of HR after meeting with the

CEO of the Americas. This time, the Head of HR, Mrs. Birr, contacted me at the recommendation of the CEO.

"Mr. Adams, I was told to speak with you regarding our search for a CFO."

She seemed to want to speak with me with as much enthusiasm as someone about to go to the dentist for a root canal. She awarded me the search and said,

" Show me what you can do."

I was determined to make a great impression.

Our communication was purely via phone. She did not want to have an in-person meeting with me. I began my search with all the enthusiasm and skills I had. Within one month, I successfully closed the CFO position. She then gave me another senior role in

Operations. Again, I was able to fill it within several weeks. After the second completion, I offered to buy her lunch. She refused and said she wasn't big on meeting the recruiters she spoke with. She also was very formal with me, constantly calling me Mr. Adams. I wasn't accustomed to such formality, so I told her

"Why don't you call me Len, and I will call you Susi."

She replied, "No, I prefer to call you Mr. Adams, and you will call me Mrs. Birr."

"Okay," I replied.

I thought this would be a two-placement relationship that would end soon. Was I ever wrong. As she built the banks infrastructure, she continued to provide me with numerous open jobs to fill. Fortunately, I closed 90% of them.

She once asked me,

 "Where have you been all these years?

She was previously the head of HR at another bank for years. She would never give me the time of day.

 I replied, "I have been right here all along but could never get you to answer my calls."

 "Well, shame on me," she replied. "I am sorry I didn't work with you sooner."

    I was on cloud nine. That was the highest compliment anyone had ever given me. I was determined to give her 150% of my effort. What ensued was a longstanding relationship that lasted until she retired some ten years later.

She also had an unusual way of dealing with recruiters. She always had numerous positions to fill. She maintained relationships with three or four recruiters, giving each of us two or three jobs simultaneously on an exclusive rotating basis. This meant that if I were given a position, it was mine to fill. Then, she would rotate additional positions to the other recruiters. We all knew each other as competitors and were OK with the arrangement.

She was also always swamped and challenging to reach during the day. Early in our relationship, she lamented that there were not enough hours to complete everything. She was also a bit of a workaholic. When she told me that, I said,

"No need to try and cram it all into the day. If you need to speak with me about a job, provide candidate feedback, or schedule interviews, I will happily give you my home phone number. Call me anytime".

 "I couldn't possibly bother you like that," she replied.

"Mrs. Birr, if I didn't mean it, I wouldn't offer it."

Well, she took me up on it. Many nights, right before or after dinner, I would receive a phone call from her. Often, my wife would answer the phone and hear,

 "Mrs. Adams, I am so sorry to bother you, but is Mr. Adams available?"

Trust me, I ALWAYS made myself available to her. I can't tell you how many jobs I wrote on a napkin because I wasn't prepared for an unexpected call. We had an excellent relationship. She sent me gifts when my children were born and was always very kind.

One day, she asked me for a favor. Her son was graduating from college. He had completed a master's and bachelor's program in 5 years. He wanted to get into banking. I pulled out all the stops and contacted some senior people at the other banks I had relationships with. I pitched him to the CEO of one such bank. They agreed to meet with him. They hired him on the spot. Mrs. Birr was eternally grateful and never forgot how I helped her son. He and I also became friendly. As a postscript, I must mention that she finally agreed to meet me for lunch the week she retired. We maintained a friendship until her passing. Unfortunately, when she retired, the bank bought another large US bank and became a large, structured institution with a short memory of all the success I had with them. I could never develop the same relationship with any of her successors. I did have a good run, however!

This success further motivated me to specialize in the niche of foreign banks opening in NY. However, I also found that many times, by the time the American Banker picked up the story of a bank seeking a license to open in NY, I was sometimes too late. Another firm was already providing recruitment services. I needed to find out earlier who was coming in and when.

Once again, my instinct kicked in. I figured out that any bank that wanted to establish an operation in New York needed to apply for a banking license. This license was generally granted by the NYS Banking Department or other regulators, depending on their desired license type. I also learned that these filings were public information. I figured out how to access this information. Having this information, I would approach Senior management in the head office to offer our services. I admit that I was not the only firm that did this. Sometimes, the head office executives were not responsive. However, I did pick up several bank clients using this method.

While continuing to focus on start-ups, I realized there must be a more efficient approach. I pondered this and realized that when these banks are establishing, they need various other services such as real estate, accounting, legal, etc.

I began researching the most active players in legal services, real estate, and other fields. Fortunately, I had already developed friendships with some major players who provided me with the necessary information.

One such relationship yielded a very successful outcome. I was friendly with a successful couple who were commercial real estate brokers in NY. We would frequently meet for lunch or coffee and speak about the market, who was coming in, etc. In

March of 1986, I was home on the weekend., celebrating my son Matthews's first birthday. I received a call from my real estate friend, who told me he had heard that the General Manager of a major European bank was in town looking at space.

"You didn't get this from me, but he is at the Waldorf Astoria Hotel until next Friday."

Armed with this information, I called the Plaza, asking for the person whose name I was given. While he was friendly, he was a bit dubious.

"How did you get my name and where I am staying," he asked.

I replied, "I am a headhunter, and getting information is what I do."

"Are you free for breakfast tomorrow? "He asked.

"Of course, "I replied.

I met with the gentleman on Monday morning at the Waldorf Astoria Hotel. Despite our cultural differences—he is a prominent politician in Europe, and I am a kid from the Lower East Side—we hit it off. We spent a great deal of time at that breakfast. He agreed that we would meet on his next trip to NY in a few weeks.

As promised, he contacted me after a few weeks, and we again met for lunch. I asked him questions about his plans for the bank, how he would build it, his marketing plan, etc. Since I am naturally curious and have exceptional interview skills, I broke the ice by asking him about his family, whether they would relocate here, and the ages of his children. After finishing lunch, we started walking down Park Avenue. As a result of the questions I asked, I discovered he was bringing his wife and two young children to New York. I offered to provide him with any information he needed since he and his family would be new to the city. As we crossed Park Ave, he stopped dead in his tracks, looked at me, and said.

"Since I have been here, I have been approached by vendors of numerous services. I have been offered sports tickets, ski trips, etc., to give them my business. You are the only one that has offered me friendship. We will be great friends, and you will have my business".

I was taken back because my offer was not a ploy but just an offer to be helpful. At that moment, I learned what I always knew: My best approach was just to be me. We did a great deal of business together for several years and developed a wonderful friendship. I was also humbled to have been the only recruiter invited to the bank's opening party at the Plaza Hotel. It was a black-tie affair with many dignitaries in attendance.

I won't bore anyone reading this with my additional successes throughout the 80s, but this was how that decade continued. I researched, pitched, and obtained a lot of clients. Many also turned me down, but I had enough to keep me busy and build the business.

****

While I had generally positive experiences, I did encounter several negative incidents with clients and candidates.

One memorable experience was connected to a search I was involved in for a Chief Trader for a European bank. I approached several potential candidates on behalf of this institution. One candidate seemed to be a good fit. After my pitch, he asked me to divulge who the client was. My standard practice was never to divulge the clients name until I had the resume and was ready to submit it. This candidate was insistent that I tell him who the client was. I was not on retainer and was reluctant to tell him. Since he appeared to be a good fit. I broke my own rule and divulged who the client was. He thanked me and said he would get back to me with his resume. For several days, I could not get him on the phone. He was utterly ghosting me. This was before ghosting became a thing.

Several weeks passed, and my client told me to stop searching since they filled the position. As was my usual practice, I asked him who they hired. I wanted to see how I may have missed someone. When they told me the name, I almost vomited. It was the candidate I divulged the name to. I told the client this, but they couldn't care less. Unfortunately, I did not have the same close relationship with them as I had with other clients. When I hung up, I called the candidate; he smugly told me he did what he had to do and approached the client directly. I told him he essentially took the food from my children's mouths. I also told him what I thought of him. I angrily told him our paths would cross again. He was utterly ambivalent and thought he was ahead of the game.

Karma does exist, however. Several years later, he was unemployed and called me to ask for my help. When he did, I asked him if he remembered me. He didn't! I was so insignificant to him that he stepped on me and didn't remember. I calmly reminded him.

I did have a search that he may have been suitable for, but I didn't trust him. I told him I was not interested in speaking with or representing him to clients. I suggested that he not call me again. I was unsure if I was right or wrong, but I had to follow my instinct. That experience shaped a policy that I have followed since... I NEVER divulge who my client is until the resume has been submitted. They can always turn down the interview if they are not interested. We also advise our clients that we do not divulge their identity to potential candidates until and unless they, the client, are interested in interviewing the candidate.

Another quick horror story involves losing a client for a reason that did not become apparent for several months. I was one of several firms that provided temporary operations staff to a mid-sized European bank. One day, my HR client at the bank, with whom I had a good relationship, called me and said,

"Len, we need to talk."

When I asked her why, as she sounded somewhat ominous, she told me they needed to terminate my contract and services, and all my temps would be terminated.

"Why?" I inquired.

She told me the head of operations complained we were too expensive. This made no sense to me because the market was transparent, and I knew market rates.

"Is the bank looking to renegotiate?" I asked

She said, "No; they just wanted my services and temporary staff terminated."

I was devastated. I couldn't figure out what had happened. I knew my prices were not out of line. As was my usual style. I shook it off and went on looking for more clients.

Several months passed, and I received a call from the same HR manager, telling me they wanted to bring back our temps at our previous rates. I asked her what happened. She said something had occurred internally that she couldn't discuss.

The great thing about NYC is that it is a large city where information is easy to ascertain. I discovered that the person in charge of Operations who made that decision was closely connected to another recruiting firm. He had a close relationship with them and had a special arrangement with them.

Before the popularity of direct deposit of paychecks, temporary staff would receive their paychecks by picking them up at the Recruiting firm's office. The alternative was a service that we and other firms provided; we would have them delivered to the client site for distribution.

The Operations Manager at that bank was responsible for receiving and distributing paychecks to the temporary employees. One week, the Operations Manager was absent due to illness. When the manager's superior received the paycheck packet, they discovered an extra envelope with the operations manager's name. Upon opening it, they found a significant amount of cash inside. Unfortunately, the absent manager failed to notify the temporary firm about his absence. This resulted in his immediate termination when the situation came to light. The firm he was taking kickbacks from was also promptly terminated.

A week later, the former head of operations, whom I had known for many years, approached me asking for help with his resume. Despite our long history, I made the rare decision to decline. He was one of only two individuals I have ever turned down during my career.

103

I have one more similar story. I had placed many people with another European bank and staffed entire departments. One day, I was uptown visiting clients. I happened to be near this client's office. I called my client, the General Manager, and told him I was near his office and would like to stop in to say hello. He was agreeable, and I told him I would be there shortly.

When I arrived at the bank, the receptionist asked me to wait a few moments. The trading room happened to be located Just outside the reception area. I placed most of the traders as well as the Treasurer. They waved me into the trading room to chat for a few minutes when they saw me. It was after trading hours, so not much was going on.   I spoke with them for a few minutes when the GM's Assistant came in to get me. She told me to please follow her, which I did. She proceeded to escort me off the premises. When I asked her where her boss was, she said he wanted me to leave the premises.

Why?" I protested.

"Please just leave," she told me.

I attempted to call this General Manager unsuccessfully. The traders had no idea what had happened.

I later discovered that the executive assistant was collaborating with another firm and attempting to provide them with business. She told her boss I was poaching employees and collecting resumes in the trading room. Nothing could have been further from the truth.

Truth be told, all the people I had placed there were there for many years. When this information about his executive assistants' plans came to light, the general manager, being very proud, did not have the face to reach out to me.

Years later, when the bank was celebrating its 10th anniversary of opening in NY, I received an invitation to the anniversary party. When I received the invite, I was sure it was a mistake. When I inquired, I was told that it was not a mistake. The GM knew he was wrong, and this was his way of apologizing. When I saw him at the party, we shook hands, hugged, and never spoke about it again. I lost ten years of opportunities but felt vindicated, knowing I did nothing wrong.

Chapter 11

Getting It Done

I was able to use my creativity to change the direction of the business by taking on additional responsibilities. The company shifted focus away from handling only back office and clerical positions. We added executive search, and specialized temporary and interim management positions. With this transition, we realized the need to improve our marketing efforts. Since we did not have a marketing brochure, I created one. I also developed a specialized industry salary survey that became widely used by clients as a source of information. I took it upon myself to do whatever was necessary to get things done. Subconsciously, I think I constantly tried to prove my value to my uncle for his approval.

I even handled issues that weren't my responsibility. One such example was when our import-export recruiter placed a candidate with a client, who ignored our invoices. When I heard about this, I asked my uncle to let me handle it. He agreed.

I made several calls to the client, but they did not respond. My plan B was to visit the client and demand payment. I asked a team member from our insurance desk to accompany me to the client's office in the WTC. When we arrived at the office, we asked the receptionist to show us to the executive's office. She told me he was too busy to see us. I was not one to take no for an answer, so I politely told her we were going in anyway. When we walked in, he was on a phone call. I asked him to please hang up the phone as we had business to discuss. When he hung up, I explained who I was and that we were there for our overdue payment.

He smugly looked at me and said,

"What if I don't pay?".

I turned to my colleague and told him to please grab the nearest typewriter, and I would grab the copy machine. The executive asked me what I was doing. I told him if he wouldn't pay in money, I would take our fee in equipment. This is an excellent time to explain that I am not a tough guy nor large in stature. In addition, my colleague was about 100 lbs. soaking wet. But he went along with my improvised plan. The executive started to get up from his chair. It seemed like he was getting up for a while because I found myself looking up at a massive man of about 6 feet 4 inches, towering over my 5'9" frame.

"I will throw you out of that f*cking window if you try to leave with any of the equipment," he angrily said to me.

As his face was breathing down mine, with my legs shaking and almost crapping my pants, I knew I had to think fast. I asked him if he owned the company. He told me he was a partner.

"Good," I said. "You realize that if you touch one hair on my head, I will sue you for assault, and I will own your company. And I have a witness."

Thankfully, he rethought his position. I calmly explained to him that our firm provided services, we had a contract, and we just wanted what was due. I am happy to say that we walked out of that office with a check in full payment of our invoice. My colleague asked me what I was going to do if he hit me. I told him I would have passed out since I was not much of a fighter. I knew, however, that I just had to get his attention and let him know we were serious.

In all my years in business, both with KPA and in my own business, I have NEVER LOST A FEE.

I always assumed the responsibility of exploring and implementing new tools, software, and websites without being asked. I would make a business case to my boss and explain how the ideas would benefit the business. Most of the time, he would agree with my proposals. This autonomy made me feel like I was running the company, even though it wasn't mine.

Chapter 12

Competition... Friend or Foe?

Early in my career, I always kept an eye on my competitors. There is a line from the great movie The Godfather that says, "Keep your friends close and your enemies closer." Although I never considered my competitors enemies. We were all vying for a share of a market that was big enough for everyone. I always followed what my competition was doing and tried to be better. Some of my best ideas came from observing them. That's just how business is. In my early years in the business, many recruiting firms were physically located in the same buildings in downtown and midtown Manhattan. We often bumped into each other at restaurants, bars, and elevators. We were all members of the professional industry associations. There was a strong sense of camaraderie among us. We would exchange intelligence on what was going on in our niche markets. We would never betray any client or candidate's confidence or confidential information. It is somewhat gratifying to know that sometimes, we were all experiencing the same issues, challenges, and successes. I believe that competition, if handled correctly, is healthy. It keeps everyone on their toes and reduces complacency. I was honored to be considered a competitor by people with many more years of experience than I did. I formed long-lasting friendships with almost every competitor I had.

I have an amusing story about a long-time agency owner and myself. Al Streuli operated independently and was known for his meticulous process. Although we had never met, we found ourselves competing on several deals. One day, I received a call from a client who was giving me a position to fill. As was my practice, I inquired if he had approached anyone else with the position. He mentioned that he had tried to reach Al, but his phone was busy. He planned to call Al again after our conversation. Upon receiving a job request, I would immediately go through candidate files and make calls to pitch the job. Since I acted quickly, I dived into the opportunity, conscious of the impending competition. I identified a few potential candidates and immediately called them. One was a great match, and he granted me permission to present him. Before faxes and emails, calling the client to introduce the candidates was customary. I immediately contacted the client and scheduled an interview for the following day.

Al reached out to the same candidate 10 minutes after I did but was told I had already spoken with him.

As luck would have it, that evening, I attended a meeting of the Association of Personnel Agencies of New York APANY, now known as APCNY, the professional association I was a member of. Al happened to be at my table that night. One of the other attendees at the table turned to Al and said,

"Have you met Len Adams? You and he are in the same niche."

Al almost spit out his drink when he saw me. I was only 25, and he was probably over 45 or 50 at the time.

"You are a baby!" he exclaimed. "And you beat me on a referral today."

He didn't say it mean-spiritedly; I think he was surprised at my youth. We shook hands, and I told him,

"Mr. Streuli, I know I am young, but may I give you some advice?"

"Sure," he said.

"You might want to get a second phone line so clients can get through and not get a busy signal."

Al and the whole table rolled with laughter. He and I became great friends and collaborated on numerous deals. I have been fortunate to have this kind of relationship with many people who were in the same industry as me.

I won't tell you that this is always the case with every competitor. Some are just cutthroat. There is a big difference between competing and being cutthroat. Don't get me wrong, I want the deal as much as the next guy. Sometimes, however, you must step back in the candidate's or client's best interest. I would never denigrate anyone else's practices. I learned not to stoop to other people's lows and always try to stay above the fray. So, friend or foe? They are usually friends unless they decide to be a foe.

I have had situations where some unscrupulous competitors have stooped to bad-mouthing, kickbacks, etc. That does not keep an industry healthy or productive for clients. Anyone can play dirty. It takes fortitude to play nice.

My training, achievements and setbacks, and recognition by my competitors defined my early career experience. I carried all of these into subsequent decades.

Chapter 13

Hiring and Firing: A Cast of

Characters

When I started at KPA, the cast of characters employed there would make the old TV show The Office look like a drama series.

Uncle Tony oversaw hiring employees for the firm. I'm not sure what his criteria were, but there was always a group of colorful characters as employees.   I can't say they were all bad, but many were unique. We also experienced a lot of staff turnover, which was common in our industry.

One of my first colleagues was a recruiter named Frank. Frank's true profession and passion were entertainment. He was a singer who performed at weddings and nightclubs. For him, this job wasn't a career; it was a way for him to pay his basic expenses while he built his singing career. He had a good voice which ultimately enabled him to leave the business to develop his wedding band into a sustainable career. He was a character, however. He was always full of jokes and stories.

Frank was getting ready to leave one Friday afternoon to perform at a club. In proper Frank form, he went into the bathroom to change into his tuxedo. He came out of the men's room in his boxer shorts, shadowboxing in the empty waiting room. We all thought it was hilarious. In the middle of his shadowboxing, he received a call. He sat at his desk to take the call while still wearing his underwear. The rest of us loudly talked about how crazy he was and how funny it would have been if someone walked in. At this point, Frank puts his call on hold, raises his hand, and yells to all of us,

"Guys, I am on a call. Can we act a little professional?"

You can't make this stuff up.

Frank was cast in the movie, The Godfather, as the wedding singer, but his scene was ultimately cut. The story goes that Al Martino, another singer in the film, did not want Frank to perform. This missed opportunity was a disappointment for Frank. When my wife and I married, we hired Frank's band to perform at our wedding. Frank was a friend, and I was always loyal to my friends.

Jeff was another team member who worked in the Steamship and Transportation industries. He was a real character who liked to go for a drink at the end of the day. When I came of age, we became great drinking buddies. He previously worked with my father outside the industry, so we developed a bond.

Jeff and I used to occasionally go for drinks at the end of the day. One Christmas, we went out before the holidays and had several drinks. As we were leaving, Jeff looked at me and meant to say, "Give my regards to your family." Instead, he said, "Give your regards to my family." We laughed hysterically. One year later, we repeated our holiday tradition of having a celebratory drink or three. As we left, he looked at me and made the same mistaken comment. We had to be picked up from the floor from laughing. Jeff was an interesting guy with a decent following of clients and candidates. However, after several years, some personal issues caused him to leave the industry. We remained friends until he died a couple of years ago.

Several years later, we had another employee named Mary. Mary was a mature woman who was brilliant. In another life, she may have been an English teacher. She was hired to help with the temp business that my uncle started in the late seventies. She would get into the office before 8 am. She would handle correspondence, some billing, and general office administration. She would do this from 8 am until 12 noon. At precisely noon, she would leave for lunch. When she returned at 1 pm, she would be completely drunk. It was impossible to complete any coherent tasks. My uncle didn't have the heart to let her go. Not to mention, what she achieved in her first 4 hours of the morning was fantastic.

One day, I was coming back to the office and observed Mary as she was coming back from lunch. Two Japanese tourists stopped her and asked her,

"Can you direct us to the World Trade Centre?"

Mary looked at them cockeyed and, without missing a beat, replied.

"You had no trouble finding Pearl Harbor, didn't you?

She turned and walked into the building, leaving the two tourists scratching their heads.

Here's one more noteworthy Mary story: One Wednesday at noon, Mary left for lunch as usual. She did not return at 1 p.m. as normal, and we were all concerned about her. We attempted to call her house that week but to no avail. We didn't call the police because we assumed terrible news would spread quickly. We were confident we would have heard if something had happened to her.

She finally returned the following Wednesday at precisely 1 p.m. Mary walked in, sat down, and finished typing where she left off a week earlier. We all looked at her and asked her what had happened. She had no idea she had been gone for a week. We all assumed she must have had a drunken blackout.

My uncle continued to put up with her for a while before finally deciding he had enough. She was becoming a liability, so he let her go. He was not fond of firing people, and after Mary, he delegated that task to me. I even had to fire employees he hired directly. That was the most uncomfortable part of my job, causing me to have to develop a thick skin.

I was not involved in any of those hires.

We had several genuinely talented people, and I enjoyed a good relationship with them. Unfortunately, not all of them were cut out for the business.

In the late 1980s, as I gained more trust from my uncle, I was allowed to change our hiring practices. I planned to hire recent college graduates and train them for long-term careers. I also intended to bring in part-time help to find employees who would commit to the business, as I had done. My goal was to reduce our high turnover rate and create a more stable staff. I aimed to hire an "anchor recruiter" with experience in banking or another related industry to bring deep industry knowledge and maturity to our office. I wanted to build a professional team of employees that we could develop.

Tony gave me some leeway but had to approve every hire. He rarely overrode me, and I had a good track record of hiring talented individuals. While I did have a few "duds" through the years, I generally had a great team of people.

I also found great success in hiring aspiring actors and actresses to make calls and research candidates. We were flexible with their schedules for auditions. They were mostly very personable, dependable, and excellent employees. Sometimes, the acting career would be put on hold or forgotten entirely. I had this happen several times. I was always very fortunate in my ability to spot talent and help develop it.

One of my favorite and most amusing stories concerned one of my early hires. In 1987, I hired a college student named Nancy Dicaro to assist in the office. On her first day, I explained that I wanted her to screen my calls. When the phone rang, she answered it, turned to me in a loud voice and said

"LEN, YOU HAVE A CALL ON LINE 1"

I didn't think much of it and chalked it up to her nervousness on her first day.

When the phone rang again, she answered it and yelled to me that I had a call. After I finished the call, I went over to her and asked her very calmly.

"Why are you screaming at me?"

She replied

"You told me to Scream the calls."

After I stopped my laughter, I explained to her that I said SCREEN, not SCREAM.

Nancy turned out to be a great employee and excellent assistant. She was like a sponge when it came to learning. Although she left after a few years, we have stayed in touch and always laugh about her first day.

I am fortunate to have developed long-lasting friendships with nearly everyone I worked with, friendships that endure for years even after they have moved on.

Chapter 14

What, Me Worry?

In the 1990s, I experienced significant changes and personal growth. I was raising three children. I juggled a busy schedule with school plays, little league, soccer, and more. I had a great team at the firm, and we were achieving good results. I was still building the business and a reputation. I generated significant revenue and was paid a minimal amount relative to my production. Don't get me wrong. I was making a living.

I was paid a bit more than some of my friends who went into civil service or education, but I was functioning in a world where I could not compete financially. I did an excellent job of hiding my financial insecurity. I was interacting with people so far ahead of me financially that I almost felt like a fraud.

I always liked to dress nicely so I looked successful. I was fortunate to always be able to find a deal or connection to buy nice clothes at a discount. My wife took a job while my children were in school to help manage our household expenses. She was excellent at stretching our money. When times were challenging, I used credit cards excessively and refinanced my house to manage my debt.

Whenever I broached the topic of money with my uncle, he assured me I was building my future.

He used to tell me,

"What does it matter if you get the big money now or at the end of the rainbow?

Remembering how my grandfather sold the family business out from under my father, I once asked my uncle Tony if he had plans to do the same thing. He was indignant in assuring me that he was not like my grandfather and had no plans to do that. This reassured me that I was building for my future. Some might think I was foolish to put myself in the financial position I was in. I truly believed I would get out of financial trouble if I continued building the business. Burying myself in producing was my coping mechanism.

Living in a fantasy world, I believed I would achieve financial stability. Despite wanting and needing money, it was never solely about money. Money was just a means to an end. My true motivation and passion were always to provide superior service to candidates and clients. The revenue I generated was a boost to my ego, constantly breaking my own production records.

Chapter 15

Moving To the Next Level

By 1992, the company had outgrown the space, we occupied, and the building had further deteriorated. It was not a place I could bring clients to. Whenever I had a client or candidate visit, I would spend my first 10 minutes apologizing for our office. Fortunately, most people were ok with it due to our reputation.

The final straw was when the central air conditioning broke. When we brought it to the landlord's attention, he suggested we replace it at our expense. He did not offer any credit or rent rebate. He wanted the firm to spend $ 10,000 on an air conditioner to improve HIS space. To add insult to injury, he was only willing to give us a one-year lease. That made no sense. I suggested to my uncle that we explore moving. The office space market was a little depressed, so I thought the time might be opportune for a space upgrade. He agreed to let me look for space. In addition to business development, recruiting, and managing the staff, I was tasked with finding space—another challenge I accepted. I looked at numerous buildings. Several would not take us. The landlords in other buildings. were concerned about the potential of additional foot traffic they thought a recruiting firm would bring. The fact was, we saw candidates by appointment only. The foot traffic was minimal.

We were turned away from several buildings. One building had a couple of recruiters and numerous criminal defense attorneys, which I thought was quite humorous. I asked the building manager why he was more comfortable having murderers and criminals walk through his building as opposed to professionals seeking new jobs. After some consideration, he agreed to lease us space.

We were able to negotiate a decent deal with some buildout. The boss was happy with the deal.

With a new lease in hand and a plan to move to 150 Broadway in September 1993, many details needed to be handled. If you have ever heard the saying, "If something can go wrong, it will," I can honestly say I did. I take full responsibility for some of the mistakes, some avoidable, some unavoidable.

We designed the space to have a bullpen with partitions, a reception desk, a private office for me, and a file room.com/kitchen. As such, we needed to buy new office furniture.

I found a furniture dealer via the New York Times. He invited me to the showroom to pick out furniture. I chose what we needed based on our floor plan. He asked for a 50% deposit. This didn't seem unreasonable. We scheduled the delivery for the Friday before Labor Day weekend. Here is where life takes you where you don't want to go. On the Thursday before Labor Day weekend, my father-in-law passed away. My wife was the youngest of 5, with a large age difference between her and her siblings, so this was a very emotional time for my wife. I was also quite upset since I had a great relationship with him. My father-in-law was very good to me, my wife, and my kids.

The furniture delivery was scheduled for the following day. Committed and dedicated, I went to the new office the next day to await the delivery. I'm sure my wife wasn't happy about it, but she never said a word. So, I went in on Friday morning to wait for the delivery. We had already moved the files and had the phones hooked up.

I arrived at the new space early. The delivery did not show up at 9:30 a.m., and the same was true for 10 a.m. I tried to reach the furniture company. I kept calling them. Finally, Dave, my furniture contact, answered. He told me the trucks broke down. He told me not to worry; they would be there. Well, by 2 p.m., I realized I had been scammed. I was unable to reach Dave on the phone.

I had to stay strong to provide emotional support to my wife. We had to get through the weekend until Tuesday to attend my father-in-law's wake and funeral.

Wednesday morning, however, it was back to solving all the problems we had. I needed to get furniture, keep business going, AND find this sleazeball who scammed me. To my uncle's credit, he didn't give me a hard time about the money we lost. Fortunately, it was not enough to hurt the business financially. It was, nevertheless, a loss, and I took it personally. I spent every spare minute tracking him down. Since I always asked many questions, I knew what town the scammer lived in in New Jersey. I contacted the local police, who told me that he was known to them as a con artist. With this information and some ingenuity, we were able to go after him for federal mail fraud since his dealings were via the mail. We were able to get some of the money back. This eased the pain a bit.

We ultimately settled into the space with a much more professional look. Since it was a little more space than we needed, I was able to sublet a portion of it to another recruiting firm. With the subtenant, the new rent was slightly more than the previous one. Plus, we were in a better environment. I was more determined than ever to grow the business now even further.

Chapter 16

Networking, Networking, and More Networking

In keeping with my routine of reading as many publications as possible, I read a story in Crains, NY, about a networking group operating in NY. This story featured one of the main participants, a CPA named Roy Hoffman. Roy was a partner in the firm of Goldstein Golub and Kessler [GGK]. I was intrigued by this concept and decided to contact Mr. Hoffman. Roy was extremely courteous; in what I learned was his normal way of doing business, he invited me to meet him for lunch. When I met him, we hit it off immediately. He was about ten years older than me. We discussed the idea of forming a networking group that would be a resource to foreign companies, or any company, that wanted to establish a base in NY.

 "Great idea," "Let's do it." Roy said.

We agreed to reach out to some contacts we each had to form a nucleus of the group. Our concept was that any business setting up needed accounting, staffing, printing, legal, software, insurance, and real estate services. So, we put our heads together and invited several people to a planning meeting.

I naturally included my friend David Elovitz, the Real estate broker who fed me leads; Vincent Raniere, CEO of a software company named IDOM; Marty Egeland, owner of Carol Printing and Office Products; Ralph Solomon, an Insurance Broker;

Maryanne Millanamow, owner of an office furniture company, Jeff Gabel, an immigration attorney, Roger Barton, a corporate attorney and Dick Block, a labor attorney, and several others.

We had the core of any service or profession a business opening in NY would need. The planning meeting was very positive. We collectively decided to incorporate as International Business Group (IBG).

We scheduled a monthly breakfast meeting to discuss our business activities, exchange leads, and invite guests. Our monthly breakfast meetings were well attended, and we always had interesting people with lively and informative discussions. Invariably, at our monthly meetings, a guest would want to join. We were open to allowing guests to join if their business did not compete with any existing members. We let new members join with the executive committee's approval. That committee consisted of Roy, me, and the other founding members. We purposely kept the membership limited to 15 members. In hindsight, we should have rethought that policy.

One addition to the group was a guest named Tony Celano. Tony came to the group in an interesting way. We were promoting IBG to all the foreign chambers of commerce. Tony had attended a meeting of the Caribbean American Chamber in Brooklyn, where he happened to pick up a flyer about IBG. He reached out to me and inquired about attending a meeting. I invited him to attend. Tony was a retired police detective who was employed in the private security business for the former NYC police commissioner, Bill Bratton.

When Tony attended the first meeting, we chatted afterward and found that when he was on the NYPD, he was partners with my uncle's nephew through marriage. Having this in common enabled us to create an instant bond and trust factor. This, along with the fact that Tony was, and is, in my opinion, a good person, allowed us to develop a personal friendship. That has lasted to this day. On a side note, Tony Celano eventually became the author of seven books, and it is he who encouraged me to write my story. The point is the formation of IBG created several deep and long-lasting friendships and business opportunities.

Our group expanded our monthly meetings to include a quarterly dinner event. During these events, we would invite guests to introduce them to people within our contact base. The events took place at a private club my uncle was a member of Tiro a Segno. Tiro was known for being one of the oldest private clubs in the city. It also houses one of the oldest rifle ranges in New York. The club's membership consisted of prominent Italian American businesspeople. Since the club limited membership to only a few hundred people, Tiro was a highly sought-after venue, as it was only accessible by invitation. Recognizing the potential for business growth, my uncle saw this as a great way to attract business through IBG. We hosted these dinners several times a year, with each member responsible for inviting 5 to 10 guests. The dinners were a social event with networking mixed in. There was no pressure, just a great way to open each other's contacts to one another.

We also organized large breakfast events under the IBG banner. We invited politicians, city and state officials, and other dignitaries to speak. This helped raise the profile of IBG. With

Roy's firm being so large, he had the influence to help fill a room and attract speakers. The first breakfast event occurred on a rainy April day on the top floor of 17 Battery Place. We featured Barry Sullivan, Deputy Mayor for Finance and Economic Development for NYC, under Mayor Dinkins. Over 300 people attended, including CEOs of major corporations and politicians from the NYC Council and NYS Assembly. The event was a huge success, thanks to the collective efforts of our group and Roy Hoffman. This was just the beginning of the numerous breakfast events we organized bi-annually. The quality of events and speakers improved over time. One of our most notable events was when we were fortunate to host Senator Al D'Amato. These events aimed to bring people together, including clients and potential clients, in the company of important and influential individuals. It's worth noting that Roy never sought the spotlight during these events. We always shared responsibility for introducing the speakers and taking pictures. This significantly boosted my confidence and sense of accomplishment as a successful businessperson. As a kid growing up on the Lower East Side, I never imagined being part of this world.

I feel incredibly lucky to have been part of IBG, which helped me grow as a businessperson. I formed a strong friendship with Roy. Despite being ten years older and very successful, he mentored me and treated me as an equal. I truly appreciated our relationship. He provided valuable advice as we built IBG, emphasizing the importance of surrounding oneself with intelligent people and making one appear smart. He also stressed that introducing clients to intelligent and trustworthy individuals builds their trust in you. I took his advice to heart and applied it diligently.

As brilliant as I felt our group was, in hindsight, I realize how shortsighted we were. Remember, this was the 90s before the World Wide Web was as much of a force as it is now. At several of our monthly breakfast meetings, we discussed developing a database of our collective contacts and sharing it amongst ourselves. Our thought was if there was a specific client I or another member wanted to target, we could check this database and see if any of the members had a contact. In theory, it was a great idea.

We started implementing the process to build this database, but it became cumbersome. Databases and systems were different from what they are today. It required a great deal of programming and input, which was more challenging than any of us wanted to commit to. So, we stuck with asking for the connections at our meetings or on a phone call with each other.

Looking back, none of us were smart enough to realize how great of an idea it was. None of us were willing to turn it into a business and open it up to the business community at large. If we were, we may have been Linked In! I am not saying we had the idea first; however, as I reflect, we could have if we hadn't focused on building our individual businesses.

We operated IBG from 1993 to 2014. Unfortunately, Roy Hoffman was diagnosed with cancer and passed away. He was way too young and suffered terribly.

I would be remiss if I didn't mention how my uncle viewed this IBG entity. At first, he was all for it. I even think he was proud of how I ran with setting it up and helping to build it. I believe that as IBG started to gain some notoriety, it frightened him. I was coming into my own and was becoming my person. In some respects, he may have been right. However, the thought of not being a part of my uncles' company during that period never crossed my mind. Again, blind loyalty!

In the early nineties, besides IBG, I became more involved with another organization known as the Council on International Banking (CIB), later renamed the International Financial Services Association (IFSA). The members included all major US banks engaged in international banking activities and many foreign banks. I initially had only a minor involvement by attending some of their dinners. Some colleagues encouraged me to become more active within the organization. Traditionally, CIB/IFSA held an annual conference for all its members in the fall. The conference would invite vendors to participate in exhibit booths to showcase their products or services. It required some convincing to get my uncle to agree to the firm's participation in these conferences.

There was the cost of exhibiting, setting up a booth, and providing giveaways, not to mention the expenses for hotel and travel. The conferences were always held in beautiful resorts like Marco Island, Palm Springs, Nashville, and similar locations.

The first conference I attended was in Opryland in Nashville, Tennessee. It was my first time as an exhibitor, so I didn't know what to expect. We set up a booth to display the firm's name, printed brochures and ordered coffee cups as giveaways. Although my booth wasn't in a prime location as a first-time exhibitor, I did my best. Thankfully, two friends and fellow IBG members, Vinnie Raniere and Marty Egeland, helped me. They introduced me to people, brought participants to my booth, and made me feel comfortable.

I met several new contacts and diligently followed up after the conference. I also saw the great potential that this could have for us as a firm. I was determined that we would become a major player for this organization.

I started planning for the next conference and convinced my uncle that we needed to stay active, especially since a few competitors were there. He agreed to let me attend the following year.

During the following year, I came up with a brainstorm. My wife and I took the kids to the Boardwalk down the Jersey Shore. As we walked on the boardwalk, I saw a stuffed animal dressed in a suit with a briefcase in a store window. I turned to my wife and said,

"That looks like a banker going to work."

At that moment, it was like a lightning bolt hit me. The company was providing temporary staff to banks. That stuffed animal inspired me to coin the term" borrow a banker." When I returned to the office, I told my uncle my idea and suggested we start marketing the banking temps with the slogan "Don't just hire a temp, Borrow a banker.

He loved it. He immediately service-marked the slogan, and I was on to my next marketing concept. We were planning the conference for the fall, and I wanted a giveaway that would capture the essence of what we were selling.

I came up with the idea to create a piggy bank with our logo and Borrow a Banker slogan. We ordered a few hundred and placed them at our booth during a conference. To my surprise, they were a huge hit! People asked for more than one, and I realized they wanted them for their kids or grandkids. I was happy to give away as many as they wished. I knew they would end up in their kid's or grandkids' bedrooms. This meant the piggy banks would be the first thing they saw in their kid's room when they woke them up and the last thing they would see when they put them to bed.

I started incorporating these piggy banks into the annual conference, changing the color and adding the year to make them collectibles. They became one of the highlight giveaway items at the conference every year.

I took note that some of the more prominent exhibitors would organize lavish dinners or cocktail parties at the conference. I knew we couldn't afford to compete with them. However, by using my IBG concept and collaborating with some of my IBG partners, we decided to sponsor a party and jointly share the costs. This turned out to be very successful. We hosted these parties for many years, and each year, they were better and better. The conference participants always anticipated our jointly hosted parties.

As I continued to participate in the IFSA organization, I realized that to make a difference, I needed to be on the inside as a member, not just a vendor/exhibitor. This coincided with the organization opening membership to vendors/exhibitors. I again convinced my uncle we needed to do this since we would be looked at as equals, not just as a vendor; I will admit, notwithstanding my convincing arguments my uncle was wise enough to recognize good business ideas. So, we joined.

IFSA had numerous committees established, the purpose of which was to discuss common business issues, best practices, etc., amongst the peer members.

As I examined the various IFSA committees, I realized there were committees for almost every department in a bank except one.... HUMAN RESOURCES. This became my next challenge. I approached the officers of IFSA with the idea of organizing a Human Resources committee. Besides the obvious benefit to my firm, my pitch was that it would likely draw more participants to the conference, meetings, etc. The concept was embraced by the powers that be and proposed to the board. It was accepted. The only caveat was that I, as a vendor member, could not chair the committee. I could only co-chair. That was fine with me. At the time, the incumbent President of IfSA was a client and a friend. He enlisted a former HR colleague, who agreed to chair the committee, with me as co-chair , I was now part of the inside track.

I was now allowed to be enlisted as a speaker at future conferences and meetings throughout the year. It was a great return on our investment for the conferences. It brought credibility.

One might be wondering how my uncle reacted to all of this. He was fully supportive of these ideas. However, something interesting started to happen. After a few years of my attending the conferences alone, he insisted that he, his son, and my second-in-command attend. My uncle started to feel that I was becoming way too visible and was becoming the face of the business. The truth is, I was.

This started to frighten him, leading to his insistence on attending. It's worth noting that he did not seek nor require my permission; it was his business and money. I did not have any issue with him being there. I failed to comprehend his son's involvement, along with my second-in-command. I'll provide more details about that later. These events took place in the late 90s and early 2000s.

Chapter 17

"The Mule on The Wheel"

During my time with my uncle, he consistently told me that his children had no interest in being involved in the family business and promised me that I would be looked after. However, he was never entirely clear on what that entailed. I was naive to believe I would eventually assume business control. I didn't give much thought most of the time until I started to see things that didn't make sense to me.

My uncle had two daughters and a son. None of his children appeared to have any interest in the business. His son was an attorney who started his law career in the Queens DA office for several years before venturing into several partnerships on Staten Island.

As previously mentioned, we relocated to a new space in the early 1990s, which we found very comfortable. We had sublet one office in the space to another recruiter. That firm decided to move out. In hindsight, I am unsure if it was their decision or if my uncle told them to leave and not tell me. When that office became vacant, my uncle informed me that his son would be taking over the office as his NYC outpost, which I later realized was a way for him to get closer to the business.

About six months later, the old man, a term of endearment that the staff referred to my uncle as given his advanced age, suggested we discuss with the landlord a plan to rent a much larger space in the building. The space he wanted was almost double that we had. When I inquired about the need for expansion, as our financials didn't justify it, he insisted that it must be done.

During negotiations with the landlord, it emerged that we would not be released from our current lease despite taking more space. The landlord would only agree to let us out of the current lease if he could rent our current space after we moved out. This meant that we were facing almost double the rent for the new space, plus the rent on the existing space for up to two years or until the space was rented out. This decision didn't make sense to me, as we weren't planning to hire more people. The business hadn't experienced significant growth at that point in time. However, my uncle insisted that I follow his instructions. So, I did. However, when it came time to execute the lease, he told me to sign as COO of the company. I refused and said to him that I disagreed with the decision to sign the lease. I did not want to take responsibility for the lease. I wasn't sure if I would be held accountable if the business failed, I didn't want to take that chance. It was also a matter of principle for me.

Unlike our previous move, my uncle wanted to be involved in the office design. He met with building management to design the layout of the office. When the design was finished, he brought them to me and threw them on my desk for review. As usual, I was busy with calls. I gave the plans a cursory look, didn't notice anything unusual, and told him I was okay with the plans. He didn't need my approval. He picked up the plans and walked towards the door of my office. At the doorway, he stopped, turned to me, and asked if I was sure I was ok with the plans. This raised a red flag in my mind. I was around him long enough to know that he was trying to put something over on me. He wanted me to affirm again that I was ok with the plans. This way, I couldn't complain about the design when whatever he had in the plans went through. When I did examine the design, several things came to the forefront. The plans were a disaster. Next to my office was another small office without a door. Then there was another small office, again with no door. Next to that was a larger office with a door. In the far corner, on the opposite end of the floor, there was a massive office the size of a presidential suite. The file room and kitchen were eliminated. Instead, all file cabinets were placed in the hallway leading from the reception area. This setup didn't seem very secure. A sink and coffee pot were in the corner of the bullpen outside my office. The bullpen was arranged so that employees were crowded together. There was a reception area with two additional offices. As for my office, he cut the size in half. I didn't have an issue with that. However, I recognized that I was being given a message about my importance to the company. I was, however, more concerned about utilizing the space efficiently, so I did not make the size of my office an issue. In addition, he put a glass window on the wall that looked into the office next to mine. The other window was next to the open doorway overlooking the bullpen.

I didn't have any issues with this since I never had anything to hide regarding my actions in my office. What I did have a problem with was that he removed the door to my office. He told me I didn't need a door. I completely disagreed with him. I pointed out that sometimes I would have a sensitive phone call that required some privacy, or I would need to have a confidential discussion with a staff member. Not to mention having to interview a senior candidate who preferred some level of confidentiality. He disagreed with me and insisted that I didn't need a door. I told him I would not approve the plans as they were. Remember, the plans did not need my official approval. He insisted that the plans would be completed as he designed them. There were too many issues with this plan, so my only change was to have my door.

I had a good relationship with the building management, so I spoke with them and clarified that I needed a door in my office. I assured them I would take the blame for them not following my uncle's instructions.

I realized the reason for the plan. Moving to a larger space was necessary to accommodate his son's plan to establish his law practice in NYC. His office was the "presidential suite" The office next to him was for his associate/law partner. The remaining offices were to be sublet to help cover the increased rent associated with this move. I didn't realize that there was another agenda at play, beyond just accommodating his son's need for space in NYC. Ultimately, the landlord installed the door in my office. Although the old man wasn't pleased, he decided not to keep arguing with me, as his other agenda was more important to him. We did rent out several of the other offices. Whenever there was an empty space, I was responsible for finding someone to rent it.

Concerning his son's law practice, I was informed that he would pay rent. I was given a rent check from his son's practice to give to my uncle during the first month they opened. However, that was the only time I received a rent check from his son or his partner. I never questioned my uncle as I felt it was his business and he could do as he wished. It was not my concern.

This decision almost led to bankruptcy since the expenses were too high. I had to generate revenue, manage the team, and find subtenants for our other space and every empty space we had.

We found tenants to occupy our vacant space and every empty nook and cranny in the new space: other recruiters, an international export company, and other miscellaneous businesses rented from us. We even had one person rent a desk who wanted access to our fax machine to process flower orders. This one was a disaster that I will elaborate on later.

As far as the business, I was under more than enough pressure to produce enough to keep things afloat, so I was working harder than ever.

We had a subtenant named Angelo D'Avino, a long-time acquaintance of my uncle and me. Angelo had previously been employed by multiple recruiting firms before starting his own. We rented him an office to help him get his business off the ground. Since he specialized in insurance recruiting, which was no longer within our scope, we weren't direct competitors. Angelo was highly skilled and knowledgeable in the industry. Despite facing setbacks in his previous jobs, he was determined to make this venture a success. My relationship with Angelo goes way back to the time when I first joined my uncle's business, and he had been closely following my career progress. He was also friendly with my uncle; they frequently played golf together. As his business grew, Angelo hired more people and took on more of our excess space.

He and I had lengthy conversations about the industry, business practices, etc. I considered him to be a friend and a mentor. We shared a mutual respect. Angelo keenly observed what was happening in the business, and I am sure my uncle confided things to him. Angelo was a very decent human being with a great deal of loyalty. He would never breach a confidence by revealing anything my uncle may or may not have confided in him. However, I also believe he observed what was happening and how I was being treated.

He came to me one day and said,

"Len, you are like the mule on a wheel."

I asked him what he meant by that. He told me that I was so focused on trying to produce for my uncle Tony and run his business that I never took the time to notice what was going on around me. When I asked him to elaborate, he merely told me to pay more attention to my surroundings He would not say anything more. While I was still somewhat oblivious to his comment, I became more attentive to the events around the office.

Chapter 18

Loyalty Is Not Always a Two-Way

Street

After talking to Angelo, I realized that my cousin wasn't just practicing law at the office; he was also gradually involving himself in his father's business. It started subtly—he became friends with my second-in-command and started taking him out for golf and drinks. Since I wasn't into golf, I didn't pay much attention.

While I was away at one of the IFSA conferences, I called the office to check-in. When I asked to speak to my second in command, my bookkeeper told me that my uncle and cousin had taken him to lunch for his birthday. She told me I would not believe what was happening while I was gone. My loyal staff felt obligated to keep me informed.

My bookkeeper was a Jehovah's Witness, so embellishment and lying were not in her character. When I hung up, I reflected to myself: I had been with my uncle for 30 birthdays and was never even given a birthday card. When I returned to the office after the conference, I reminded myself to stay vigilant because something seemed suspicious.

That same week, I bumped into our landlord on my way into our office building. When he saw me, he asked if I had been away. I replied that I had been at a conference. He then mentioned that it was good I was back because the office had been chaotic while

I was gone. He described it as being "like a three-ring circus." I thanked him for the information and made a mental note of it.

I felt my uncle and cousin were preparing my second-in-command to possibly replace me. On multiple occasions my cousin introduced my second-in-command as the "person who runs my father's business" on multiple occasions, This was repeated to me from several sources. I had become the business's public face and gained substantial control over the staff and client relationships. I believe this made my uncle and cousin uncomfortable. Although my cousin claimed he didn't want to be involved in the business, his actions indicated otherwise. They both knew I had a problem with this. My issue stemmed from the fact that I had been told that the company would eventually be mine. Looking back, I realize that I was naive. I might have been fine if I had been aware of the plan. In hindsight, I understand that

174

my uncle was trying to protect his family, but I wish he had been more upfront about it. All I wanted was to be informed about his true intentions.

I noticed that the bond between my second-in-command and my cousin was getting stronger. I didn't feel the need to interfere or suspect any ulterior motives. I stayed dedicated to the business, my uncle, and my second-in-command, continuing to be the "mule on the wheel."

After seeking reassurance from my uncle about the future of the business, he once again assured me there was no cause for concern. However, when I asked him whether I would eventually become a partner with his son, he firmly replied, "Never." While I initially interpreted this as his son not being involved in the business, looking back, I believe he meant that I would not become a partner.

Still unsettled, I approached him again several months later to discuss the future of the business. He firmly assured me that everything was under control. I suggested he step back and formulate a plan to transfer ownership to me with a buyout. My offer was to buy him out by providing him with an income for the rest of his life. Furthermore, if he passed away, I would continue that income to his wife for as long as she lived. I suggested we come up with a reasonable figure for that income. He told me that would not be acceptable. Non-negotiable. This started to give me some indication that he was never going to turn the business over to me, as he had indicated for three decades.

In early 2001, I experienced several alarming incidents, although I didn't fully understand their significance at the time. I began receiving calls from some of my competitors who informed me about rumors circulating in the market that the firm was going out of business. I reassured everyone who contacted me that this was an unfounded rumor, I mentioned this to the old man, who dismissed it as nonsense. More about this later.

The second incident involved a conversation I had with my uncle Tony, months after my offer to him. He came to and told me he was planning to sign papers giving me a piece of the business. However, he had a problem. The lawyers who had the papers were involved in a plane crash overseas and died, and they had the documents with them. I asked him if there were any other copies, but he said no. I suggested that the law firm had copies. I never heard anything about those papers again. There was a plane crash involving several lawyers from the US who were traveling overseas, so that part was true. Did they have his papers? That is debatable. How naive and dumb was I?

In February of 2001, the CEO of a publicly held staffing company approached me to discuss possibly joining their team. This may have been a result of rumors in the market. Perhaps they felt the firm was vulnerable or in trouble. Throughout my career, I have received similar offers numerous times, even to this day. I have ALWAYS turned down those offers as I was completely loyal to my uncle and the company. However, this time was a bit different. I agreed to talk with them based on everything that was happening around me.

I had to ensure that I could protect my family. This was only the second time in 34 years that I had considered changing jobs. I agreed to meet with the CEO of that company. During our meeting, he explained that he had known about me for years and wanted to discuss a position as a player/coach. In other words, they wanted me to generate business and manage a team of people. Piece of cake for me.

Then, we delved into the question of compensation.

" What do you earn?" he asked me.

I explained to him that my current compensation was irrelevant since I was severely underpaid and did not reflect what my team and I produced. I explained that that was one of the reasons I entertained having a discussion with him. He pressed me for an answer. I finally gave in and embarrassingly told him what I earned. We continued the discussion for a bit. He asked me how I would structure the team. I explained that I could possibly come with my number two. I was still loyal to him even though he was probably looking to stab me in the back. At the end of the meeting, the CEO said he would get back to me.

I left the meeting not sure what to think.

After several days, the CEO of that firm called me. He told me he wanted to make me an offer. He would pay me what I was currently earning and, at the end of the year, would reevaluate what was accomplished.

"Why would I accept that?" I asked him.

I wasn't actively seeking employment. I told him that I was only open to discussing it if I could be compensated based on my performance. I proposed receiving a percentage of the revenue I generate and a modest salary for managing the team.

He countered with, "No, my offer stands."

I thanked him and explained that I could not consider what he offered and that it insulted me. My ego was also a bit bruised.

Three weeks after that discussion, my second-in-command came to my office and gave me two weeks' notice. I asked him why, and he said he had received a job offer. I then asked him the name of the firm from which he received the offer. He responded that he didn't want to divulge the name. I then told him the name of the firm

"How do you know that?" he asked.

I told him that they had approached me several weeks earlier and that I was discussing the possibility of moving and taking him with me. However, I explained that their compensation plan was unreasonable. I also mentioned that they were only hiring him because they thought he could take my book of business.

"Six months," I told him.

"What is six months? "He asked.

I told him that was how long he would last before they realized he could not move my book of business.

"That insulting," he said.

"Perhaps, but it is reality."

Six months later, to the day, he called to inform me that I was correct. They let him go when they realized he could not move all my clients away from me. I did not derive any sense of joy or satisfaction from this. I felt sorry for him for not recognizing my loyalty once again.

When I analyzed why he left us in the first place, I realized that he probably came to recognize that he was in the middle of what amounted to office politics and was coming out on the wrong side.

I found myself faced with the task of rebuilding my team, which left me feeling somewhat disheartened at the time. I remembered a saying I had read: "That which does not destroy me makes me stronger." This inspired me to remain determined to rebuild the team and keep the business going. Despite this, I remained loyal to my uncle. I found it hard to believe he wanted to downgrade my standing in the company.

Other than this one interview and the one I went on when I was first starting, I never considered not being a part of the business. I always believed that my uncle had my best interest at heart. Honestly, I probably would not have accepted the offer even if the other firm had agreed to my terms.

It felt like we were engaged in a chess match. My uncle was uncertain if I recognized what was going on, so he attempted to reassure me that we would continue the business. I was given the go-ahead to hire a replacement. Meanwhile, his son took a different approach, expressing his desire to help grow the business and assuring me that I was the key person, boosting my ego. I went along with it out of loyalty, but my instincts began to signal me to be more aware and vigilant.

I rebuilt the team and continued bringing in clients and generating revenue for the balance of 2001,

With a newly energized team and my focus back, we continued throughout 2001—that is, until September 2001

Chapter 19

9/11, The Day That Changed the World

On September 9, 2001, I flew to Scottsdale for the annual IFSA conference at the Phoenician Resort. This year, I was allowed to attend alone, as my uncle and cousin either lost interest or felt it wasn't worth spending three times the amount to have them there while I managed the booth.

The evening of September 10th, one of the banks invited me to a private dinner. It was a late night, with wine flowing freely.

On the morning of 9/11, I woke early to be at the exhibit area by 8 am. As I was dressing, I saw on the news that a plane had hit the WTC. I didn't pay much attention to it and chalked it up at that moment to a commuter plane going off course. Plus, I was a bit groggy from the night before. When I arrived at the exhibit hall, it was empty. I found some other attendees and asked what was going on. They told me that the plane that hit the WTC was not a small commuter plane but a regular airliner. The conference organizers gathered all the attendees and exhibitors into a room with a large TV screen. As we watched the events of the morning unfold, the news reports revealed that not one, but two jet airliners had hit the WTC. We then saw reports about the attempt on the Pentagon and the crash in Shanksville, Pa. Over 500 people were in the room watching these events, and the silence was deafening. As we all watched in horror, the nightmare worsened.

We observed the first tower collapse, followed by the second one.   Everyone was in shock,

To make matters worse, many of the attendees and the organization that organized the conference had offices in the WTC. Sadly, almost everyone in the room knew people whose offices were in the Twin Towers. Words cannot adequately explain the prevalent feelings in the room that day. The only way I could describe it is as follows. When one arrives at the Scottsdale Phoenician, there is a clock on the side of the building with an inscription saying: "**Where time stands still**." The statement was incredibly prophetic for all of us who attended the conference.

As we watched this nightmare unfold, everyone in the room frantically called their homes, offices, etc. Cell service was spotty due to the network's sheer volume, but we all did our best.

My first call was to my wife to ensure that she and my children were safe. She told me she had picked up our kids from school, and my daughter had come home from her classes at Wagner College on Staten Island. I was relieved to hear they were okay, but I didn't know what to expect. I advised my wife to stay home and stay safe. She told me that Scottsdale was probably the safest place I could be and suggested that I stay there. However, I couldn't fathom staying 2000 miles away from them. I promised to be home as soon as possible. Since the next day was my daughter's scheduled day to go to the office, which was one block from the Twin Towers, I instructed her not to go to the city. She informed me that I didn't realize how bad things were and that the city was closed down. No one knew when it would reopen. I then called my uncle's house to check on them and check-in.

When he answered the phone, he was frantic.

"This is going to put us out of business. How can we operate?" he said nervously.

I told him the whole world would be shut down for the next few days. I guaranteed I would find a way to get home quickly and protect the business. I tried to assure him calmly and confidently that I would take care of everything. I then reached out to my team to ensure they were ok. They were in the office that day but were safe. Some had difficulty commuting home but found solutions. I told them not to worry, to stay home the next few days and stay safe. Everything would be ok. Now, I needed to figure out what to do.

All of us at the conference were in the same situation. All planes were grounded for the foreseeable future. Somebody in our group came to us and said they had found a local bus company that we could hire. That bus would take 50 of us across the country for $100 per head. This sounded like a good deal. We agreed to meet with the owner of the bus company. When the owner, whose name was Bubba, showed up, I didn't get a warm and fuzzy feeling about him. Red flag number one. We asked him about bathrooms, bathroom stops, meal stops, etc. He was vague in his responses and said we were in his hands not to worry. Red flag number two. He then told us he wanted to be paid in total upfront. Red flag number three. Several of us were concerned and voiced this to the rest of the group. We countered him with a plan to pay 50% when he showed up in the morning and the balance when we arrived in NY.

"Nope," he said. All upfront now or no go."

Several of us protested. I think our NY sense told us something was wrong. We were overruled. Someone in the group collected the $100 from everyone. Even though it was against my better judgment, I agreed to go along with it. We planned to meet him in front of the hotel at 6 am the following day. We all proceeded to pack and check out of the hotel for the next day. The hotel was accommodating, providing us with pillows, water, blankets, and so on for our journey. The following day, Wednesday, 50 of us stood at the front of the hotel with luggage and the supplies provided by the hotel. At 6 Am. No Bubba. 6:15 am. No Bubba. I started telling everyone,

"He is not coming."

Everyone told me I was being negative, insisting he must be stuck in traffic.

"At 6 am in Scottsdale, Arizona, traffic?" I exclaimed

We waited until 7 AM and started calling Bubba, all calls went unanswered. When we finally got Bubba to respond, he gave us a story about the government confiscating his bus for the military. We asked him about our money, and he said he would try to get it back. Even though we only lost $100 each, I was unwilling to let it go. I know Bubba was banking on a group of businesspeople with expense accounts, not being concerned about a measly $100. However, for me, it was personal.

I never take it well when someone tries to take advantage of a bad situation, and this circumstance was no exception. We called the local police and explained what happened. We learned that Bubba was known to them.

One police officer told us,

"He is halfway to the casinos now. "

Nevertheless, we encouraged the police to follow up on finding him and were willing to press charges.

Several of us rented a van and decided to drive cross-country to get home. Before we left, however, I needed a plan to recoup our money.

One of the people in attendance was a guy I knew well who attended the same high school, as me. Since we were leaving with our rented van and he was staying another day, I reminded him that we were New Yorkers and to remember that we don't let anyone take advantage of us. He promised to follow up with the police and to get our money back. I trusted that he would do so. True to his word, my friend recovered everyone's money, and we sent everyone back their $100 when we returned to NY.

It was a small win in a horrible situation. As far as getting home, the 5 of us who rented the van began our trek cross-country from Arizona to New York. We left on Wednesday afternoon, alternating drivers and taking turns napping in the back of the van. We made three stops: one for a quick dinner Wednesday night, breakfast Thursday morning, and dinner Thursday night. We opted to drive through the night rather than make any hotel stops.

We were all anxious to return to our loved ones and businesses. Every stop we made for meals and fuel reinforced our faith in humanity. When the restaurant or gas station discovered we were New Yorkers, they could not have been more gracious and accommodating. They allowed us to charge our phones, wash up, etc. In any case, we made it cross country in record time, arriving in New York by Friday morning.

After hugging my wife and kids when I arrived home Friday, I contacted my uncle again. He was still panicking about what would happen with business. I promised him that I would get things under control.

Since the entire downtown area south of Canal Street was closed for an undetermined amount of time, I knew we would not return to the office for a while. So, I formulated a plan. The first thing I did was to have a message on our website that we were available remotely and would be available for any questions. Next, I contacted the phone company and had them temporarily forward calls to my second line in my house. By Monday, I had my staff on standby in case we needed to speak with clients or candidates. Since everything was shut down, there wasn't much we could do. Every other business and competitor were in the same situation By the end of the following week. I was able to make a trip to the office. It was like a war zone. The armed military allowed people with identification to get into their offices for a very short time. I was able to get our backup tapes and any other material, phone numbers, records, etc., that would help keep us in business. I must admit that it was not very pleasant going to NYC. The downtown area reeked of a dreadful odor, and an eerie feeling of death hung in the air. I remember the smell and the eeriness to this day.

Nevertheless, I tried to remain calm to determine how we would get past this. By the second week after 9/11, we carefully started to reach out to clients and our temp employees. Many of our temps were being utilized in disaster recovery locations. The banks had to reopen, so business needed to be transacted. In addition, our temps were required to be paid, as did our staff. To my uncle's credit, everyone continued to be paid even though not much was happening. To my daughter's credit, she ensured the payroll was processed to pay our temps on time. Fortunately, we did not have any employees in the WTC. We were afraid to make calls, not knowing if anyone we knew was in the building that fateful day. Unfortunately, we did hear about some clients, contacts, candidates, and friends who lost their lives. We held our breath every time we initiated a phone call.

We made it through the several weeks it took us to return to the office. By mid-October, we were allowed back into our office building. New Yorkers are resilient, so we were able to pick up some business. In fact, from October through the end of 2001, we experienced a substantial increase in business, which generated some decent revenue.

As they say, every cloud has a silver lining. The government made grant money available to businesses and residents of the downtown area who suffered losses. Through my IBG connections, I was fortunate to have had a good contact who was an employee of The NYC Economic Development Corporation, a quasi-city government agency. She awarded us a no-bid contract to provide Temporary staff to assist with the Grant Intake and application process. As a result, our temp business increased dramatically. I was in survival mode and did what I could to keep the business going. On a side note, I mentioned the grants that the government was giving out. Fortunately, our company did not suffer any substantial economic loss. As a result, we couldn't get any government money. I bring this up because my uncle pointed out that fact to me. His exact words were,

"Look what you did."

"We can't even get any grant money because you did too much business."

That wasn't a thank you for getting the business through; it was a criticism that he couldn't access the government funds! Go figure!

Chapter 20

Post 9/11

The conversation with my uncle about not receiving grant money was eye-opening. I started to feel unappreciated. I had spent over 34 years of my life as part of his company. I treated a business that was not mine as if it was my own. I responded to clients, the staff, and him on an on-demand basis. I took minimal vacation time and yet was in a financially unstable position. I continued working because it was the only thing I knew how to do.

I was unwavering, however, in my continued efforts towards the business' success. As 2002 started, the company had its ups and downs. We had decent months and slow months. The economy was slowing down due to the instability in the world post-9/11. As a business, we had been through difficult times before. My team and I did our best to generate revenue. Despite this, the old man's complaints became worse and worse. I chalked much of it up to his advanced age of 86. I still felt that something was going on, but I could not put my finger on it.

In the spring of 2002, my friend and sub-tenant Angelo told me to watch my back again. When I asked him to elaborate, he said he couldn't.

However, he viewed me as a friend, and that's all he could say. As usual, I didn't give it much thought and just focused on producing. I figured whatever was going on would come to light eventually.

I became increasingly frustrated whenever I tried to get my uncle to commit to what would happen to the business when he retired or passed on.

His answer always was, "Don't worry about it".

I had conversations with him for years and was always told the same thing. This concerned me due to his advanced age. I was witnessing the increased presence of his son in the business. All I wanted was some clarity. I realized that his agenda and mine may not have been aligned. But again, I didn't focus on it and buried my head in the sand as I was known to do when I had a problem.

Producing and staying busy were always my escape. It was what I was good at and what I enjoyed doing. From the bottom of my heart, I always believed I would find the answers to my future.

I knew something had to change, especially since at this stage I was 48 years old. My family was getting older, and their needs were becoming increasingly more expensive. I always believed in a higher power and told myself something would break soon.

I tried to stay focused and keep my team motivated.

My uncle wasn't around much throughout the winter and spring months, and there was a strange vibe that I couldn't put my finger on. As I said, even though it was a tough economy, we still produced as best we could. I never wavered in my commitment to continue building and producing revenue. Everything was moving as usual until.............

Chapter 21

Defining Moments

"We need to get rid of your daughter." These words that my uncle said to me in June of 2002 were the beginning of the transformation of my life.

After following my uncle's orders, I knew my life was going to change. The answers I couldn't find were now coming to light.

When I returned home, obviously distraught, I discussed what had happened with my daughter and wife. We knew something wasn't making sense. Part of me wanted to not go return to the office, but the other part wanted to investigate and reach a conclusion.

I explained this to my wife and family and told them I owed it to myself to figure out what was happening and then make some decisions. I knew in my heart that I would be gone soon. I needed to figure out what his end game was and what mine would be.

I decided to go back to the office on the Monday after the July 4th holiday, this time with my eyes and ears wide open. As a professional, I showed up and performed my job as usual. Going back as if nothing happened was the best thing I could do. I knew that somehow, things would start to unfold, and boy, was I right. One of my assistant recruiters was a young lady named Janice. She was about my daughter's age. She had been on vacation the prior week. When she returned, she asked me where Heather was.

"I fired her," I told her.

She asked me why. I explained that I was ordered to. She expressed how messed up she thought that was. As I described earlier, the staff sat in an open bullpen outside my office. What happened next allowed me to figure out part of what was going on. When Janice got back to her desk, her phone was ringing.

I heard her loudly say,

"Hello, Mr. V"

The staff referred to my uncle as Mr. V, another term of endearment. Since he had hearing loss, phone conversations had to be loud for him to hear. The rest of the conversation went as follows. I could only hear the conversation from Janice's side.

"I'm fine"

"You want me to come to your house tonight?"

"And don't tell Lenny?   Ok, I will be there."

Janice knew I heard her side of the conversation, and she was very uncomfortable with what was happening. She immediately came into my office to speak to me. As I mentioned earlier, my staff and I always had mutual respect.

She asked me what was going on. With my daughter gone and Mr. V wanting to meet her without my knowledge, she knew this wasn't good.

I was already past the point of being pissed off. I was now in strategic mode. I had to let this play out as I knew a more extensive plan was afoot.

Having spent the better part of 34 years with my uncle, I understood how he thought.

"Janice, something is going on that is not making sense," I told her.

"My uncle feels I have too much control over the staff and the clients, and he has another plan to knock me down."

I figured he wanted to take control back. I did not yet know the true plan he had.

I went on to tell her

"What is going to happen is you will go to my uncle's house, and he will tell you that he wants you to be on his team and watch me"

What he was watching for is beyond me.

"He will also tell you he needs to cut your hours"

He was on a cost-cutting kick.

"His son will sit there watching TV, pretending he is not part of the conversation. When Mr. V tells you he wants to cut your hours, you will naturally tell him that you can't afford to do that. His son would perk up and say,"

"Why don't I give you some additional hours working for me? This way, you don't lose any income?"

I told her that they would then tell her not to tell me that she was there. She asked me if I thought she should go; I told her she should because he owned the business and requested that she do it. Plus, I wanted to see if my assessment of this situation was correct.

Janice went to my uncle's house as instructed that evening. The conversation went EXACTLY as I predicted. When they finished their discussion, they asked her if she had any questions. She did. She told my uncle she had been asking me for a raise, which never came through. This was true. I kept asking my uncle to let me increase her hourly rate, and he refused. My uncle told her,

"Len doesn't like to give raises."

He blamed it on me! I had ZERO authority to raise anyone's salary. Everything had to be approved by him. He told her he would give her an increase. She knew he was lying because she knew the business's setup. I managed the company in all aspects except financial dealings.

He also told her not to tell me anything.

Janice was very loyal to me. When she left his house, she immediately called me. She told me what transpired and that it was almost word for word the way I told her it would go.

"How did you know?" She asked me.

"I have been around them too many years," I replied.

She then told me that she did not want to return because she was very uncomfortable with the situation. She also did not want to report to my cousin. I told her I understood. I encouraged her to file for unemployment the next day. The form would come to the office, and I would approve it for her if I were there. She thanked me and wished me luck.

The next day, my uncle came to the office. When he looked around, he noticed that Janice wasn't in. When he came into my office, he asked me where she was. I told him she called me that morning and resigned for some inexplicable reason.

My uncle said, "Yeah, I know she called me to complain about you; I guess she was unhappy."

I knew right then and there that he was lying to me. This was like a punch in the gut. A man who I looked up to and revered for so many years was treating me like a stranger. I felt betrayed and angry. My ancestry is Jewish and Italian. The Italian blood in me wanted to jump over the desk and hit him. The Jewish side of me told me to be calm and now play him at his own game. He asked me if I had anything to say about firing my daughter. I think he was trying to bait me into an argument.

213

I explained that I did what needed to be done with his orders for the business, as I always have.

"Do you understand what is going on here? He asked me.

"I understand perfectly well," I replied.

"You give orders, and I execute them without questions asked. You are the boss, and I am the servant. I got it."

"Good," he said. " "Remember, I made you, and I own you," he said.

My reply was, "I thought Lincoln freed the slaves. 100 years ago."

I decided not to pursue that argument further. I wanted to let him feel he had won.

He advised me if we needed to hire additional staff. I agreed to reach out to find new employees, but I knew I wouldn't follow through on his request. He suggested contacting Goodwill

214

Industries as he heard they could provide employees. I had spent 34 years trying to improve and build a professional team, and now he wanted me to seek inexpensive labor from Goodwill Industries!

At that moment, I realized that he had no respect for me or everything I had done for him over the years. I no longer felt any remorse or guilt for the things he did for me. As far as I was concerned, the score was even.

I still needed to find out why, but I knew I could only count on staying there for a little while longer.

Even though I was distraught with the situation, I still had a job and clients to serve. I continued to do so. I also knew I needed to make an exit plan. Through all of this, I still did my job.

Chapter 22

A New Beginning

This whole situation led me to do a lot of soul-searching to determine my next step. I almost felt burnt out and beaten down. I wasn't even sure I wanted to continue in the industry. I knew, however, that my time at KPA was coming to an end.

I spoke openly and honestly with my wife, close friends, and business advisors. I also consulted multiple attorneys to discuss what transpired.

Everyone I spoke with encouraged me to stay in the industry. The industry was my career and what I excelled at. I was sure I did not want to be employed by anyone else. My only alternative was to find backers or money somehow to fund the business.   I told my wife my fears and reluctance; she was very supportive and told me I would be crazy to leave the industry.

"This is all you have done your whole life, and I have watched you. You are good at what you do".

After a great deal of thought, I told her that she was right.

"The only way I could do this is to take a second mortgage on the house. I don't want investors because I would be accountable to others again. So, you must understand that if we do this, we are all in. We need to give it a year."

To my wife's credit, she reminded me that we came from nothing and didn't have much, so we had nothing to lose. I explained to her that we would be back in an apartment in a year and probably bankrupt if I failed.

"I believe in you and am willing to take the chance."

I promised her that if we made it past a year, I would buy her a new, larger house. I also said that our lives would be significantly improved if we made it.

I needed to devise a plan, so I scheduled a meeting with a prominent attorney in the staffing industry who was familiar with me and my uncle. I explained the situation to him. He then inquired whether I was an officer of the corporation, to which I replied that I was not. He further asked if I had check-signing authority, to which I answered in the negative. He also asked if I had a non-compete agreement, and I informed him that I did not.

He asked me if I had any equity in the business. Once more, I told him I did not.

He said, "After 34 years of running his business, if he hasn't given you any of those things and has treated you the way he has, along with the broken promises, he doesn't deserve to have you."

He gave me some additional advice.

"Make your plan to leave on YOUR time, not company time. Do not set up a corporation or file for an LLC while employed. Do not tell any clients or candidates that you are planning to leave. I have known you for over thirty years, and you have always conducted yourself as a gentleman and a professional. Walk out with nothing but your knowledge and reputation and with your head up high.

It may hurt but do business for him until the day you leave. Do not hold back any deals. It may hurt, but you will win in the long run,".

I thanked him and decided to follow his advice to the letter.

This was around July 8. I need to set a plan and an end date. Without this, I would continue to languish there, miserable. I proceeded to apply for a second mortgage on my house. That took about two weeks. Once I had that line in place, I needed to set a day for my exit.

I told my wife that I was going to resign on July 25. I knew giving notice was not an option. I also knew I had to have a firm exit date that I was committed to; otherwise, I might change my mind. He would not want me there once I announced my plan to leave. I set that date because the summer was quiet, and I would be able to get the business started in September.

I continued to operate on behalf of KPA, even taking on new jobs and attempting to fulfill with the team.

Since it was summer, my uncle did not come in frequently. On July 24, with a great deal of angst and anxiety, I called my uncle's house. My aunt answered and told me he wasn't home. I asked her to please have him call me. He called me later that day, and I asked if he would be in the next day because I needed to speak with him. He told me he would be. Thursday came and went, and I never heard from him. I called his house Friday morning, and my aunt said he wasn't around. I told her I needed to speak with him and would even come to their house if he didn't want to come in. She told me he would call me.

On Monday, July 29, he again did not come in or call. I called him again that afternoon. He told me he planned to come in but had things to do. He promised me he would see me on Tuesday. You guessed it, Tuesday came, and he did not come in again. Deep down, I think he knew what I wanted to speak about, but as usual, he stalled me, thinking it would blow over.

I waited until mid-afternoon and called him again. He did get on the phone and asked me what I wanted. I told him that I did not want to discuss this on the phone but that since I had been trying to see him for almost a week, I was forced to do so. I told him I was resigning and did not want to be part of the company any longer My heart just wasn't in it. He started to berate me for being ungrateful and threatened to burn my house down. On the advice of an attorney, I was recording the call and advised him of that. I also knew however that he was angry at that moment and his threats were meaningless. I told him it wasn't personal; it was business. I informed him I was leaving a formal resignation letter on my desk, along with my office keys and passwords to all the computers and software programs. I also explained that on that very day, I closed a deal for a $25k fee. I informed him the candidate would be starting in two weeks. That deal interesting enough was with IFSA, the organization that we were members of and whose conferences we attended.

That was my parting gift to him. I prepared the invoice for him to send out in two weeks. I thanked him for all he did for me and wished him well.

Shaking and nervous, I left the office at 150 Broadway for the last time. I called a dear friend of mine Dick Block, who was a labor attorney. He told me to meet him at his office before I went home. I did so. Dick has known me for a long time, was part of my IBG organization, and was a trusted friend. He knew what I was going through and knew I was visibly shaken. He first told me that I was making the right move.

 "Everyone always thought you were the company owner by how you carried yourself,"

He asked me to look at him closely. He shook his head from side to side, saying, "No." He reminded me that my uncle would return to me with numerous promises of money and partnerships. He told me to visualize his head saying, "No," etc.

"Don't get weak in the knees."   He cautioned.

This was the same advice I had given hundreds of candidates throughout the years when discussing counteroffers. I guaranteed him that my decision was made. The hard part was over.

When I arrived home, my wife had made us a drink, and we both toasted to the future. We agreed to start this new journey together and never look back.

****

The following morning, I slept a little later than my standard 6:30 am wake-up time since I did not have to commute to the city.

One of my first calls that day was to my old colleague, Richard York Ullo, whom I wrote about earlier in this book. In an earlier chapter, he had gone through a similar experience with my uncle; I called him to tell him that I left. I knew he would be the only other person who could appreciate and understand what I had just experienced

"It's about time," he told me.

He asked me how I felt. I told him that it was the first time since I was 15 years old that I had nowhere to go, nothing to do, and no plans, but I felt great, as if the weight of the world had been lifted off my shoulder. I told him I was either ready to move forward or was having a nervous breakdown; I wasn't sure which.

"You are going to be fine. You are ready to come into your own. I wish you nothing but success,".

I thanked him and agreed to meet for lunch in a couple of weeks. I decided that day to start putting things in motion for a September launch. I made an appointment on Friday with my friend and attorney, Roger Barton, who handled corporate law. The purpose of my visit was to incorporate and set up the name of my company. I met with Roger that Friday, and we came up with Adams Consulting Group LLC, doing business as ACG Staffing, later changed to ACG Resources.

August 2, 2002, became the official incorporation date of the business. I use that date as my business anniversary, even though we didn't start doing business officially until September.

I had a lot on my plate - finding office space, designing and ordering business cards, obtaining phone lines, phones, and computers, opening a bank account and getting insurance. It was a large undertaking, but I was ready for the challenge. My friend and mentor, Angelo D'Avino, once told me that the secret to success is biting off more than you can chew ... and chewing it. I was chewing it!   Throughout August, I dedicated my time to getting everything in order and relied on a second mortgage to get by. It was invigorating in a way I hadn't expected. I even gave myself the title of CEO of Adams Consulting Group. LLC, a company that, at that point, consisted of one employee. Me.

****

After a week or so, my uncle contacted me, asking if we could speak to discuss what happened. Even though he turned on me, I arranged a call with him.

He began by telling me that he had a problem. He explained that he had negotiated with a buyer for the business. The problem was he now couldn't sell it without me there. Now I understood what the agenda was and what all the rumors of us going out of business were about. He explained that he and his son had numerous meetings with a firm that wanted to buy the company based on its revenue and reputation. They would pay some upfront cash and offer a five-year payout. They would add additional staff to continue to build the business. I asked him why he thought it made sense to have these discussions without me, his "COO" present.? Was it even a good look for the negotiations? He didn't admit being wrong but made me an offer to come back as President, with a raise in salary, a piece of the up-front cash, a partnership in the business, access to his country clubs, a piece of the final payout in 5 years a percentage to be determined, and attendance at all meetings with the buyer.

I politely told him that if that offer had been on the table a month earlier, I would have accepted it. At this point, I did not want to take a step back. His amounts sounded very appealing, mainly since I was living on a second mortgage and accruing more debt every week. However, I couldn't forget how he had treated me over the past year and how hurt I was to discover that he was doing all of this behind my back. I also remembered my friend

229

Dick Block, as well as the advice I had given candidates throughout my career. Never accept a counteroffer. As they say on the show "Who Wants to be a Millionaire," that was my final answer. I also remembered a great piece of advice my uncle had given me years ago when I considered taking a job in a bank. He told me to only depend on myself for my career and growth. That advice could not have been sounder.

I thanked him for the offer and told him I was sure he would figure things out. He continued to call me for several weeks with questions about how to handle specific software and other issues.

I accommodated him until I discovered he was badmouthing me to the family and people in the industry. He also put his name on various articles that I had written that were on his website. These articles were all items I wrote on my own time at night. I did not write them during the day on his time. Nor was I paid extra for them. I felt confident that they were my intellectual property and wanted credit. I was not going to give them to him. So, I asked him nicely to remove them. He did not, so I had to have an attorney send him a letter that the articles were my intellectual property and needed to be taken down. He did finally comply.

About a month after I started my business, we decided that my wife would leave her job to assist me. While it was not the most brilliant move at the time since she was earning an income, I needed some help with the phones and screening candidates. Plus, we both believed that the business would take off soon.

One day while I was out of the office at a meeting, my wife received a call from the FBI, asking her to have me call them back.

I asked her if they told her why they wanted to speak with me. They did not share that information with her. Since I knew I never did anything wrong, I returned the call. They requested we meet in my office. When we met, 2 FBI agents came in and showed me a book of pictures. They pointed to one and asked me if I knew him. The man in the picture was one of the people my uncle had rented space to. The individual told us he was selling roses online and taking orders via fax. He was using the fax to commit wire fraud, unbeknownst to us I asked what any of this had to do with me. The agent advised me he had spoken to Mr. V, my uncle, who told them it was I who rented the space to that person, and I was responsible. I explained to the agent that I merely managed the office, and in fact was no longer employed at KPA. The agent asked me who received the rent.

I was clear with the FBI agent that the rent was paid by check and made out to the company (KPA). The rent check was handed over to my uncle for deposit each month. I emphasized that I was not the owner of the business and was not involved in the finances. I also informed them that I was not an officer of the company nor was I a signatory on the bank accounts. The FBI agent apologized for wasting my time. It was frustrating to be wrongly accused of something I was not involved in, nor received any financial gain from.

My uncle did his best to salvage the business. He approached nearly every contact in the industry to find someone to take my place. Unfortunately, he struggled to attract anyone. The sale was put on hold and ultimately canceled.

After my uncle failed to attract anyone from inside the recruiting industry, he made a move that he thought would be his salvation. My brother Stephen was going through his own career crisis. My uncle and cousin approached him with the idea that he would take my place. They made him numerous promises like those made to me. They also told him that he was blood, and I wasn't so that he would be taken care of. My brother needed help, so this seemed like a good decision for all of them.

I wasn't upset that my brother took a job there; I knew it would not be easy for him to compete with me. Not for lack of skill, he didn't have the longstanding client relationships I had. I knew all the promises that were made would never be fulfilled.

My uncle tried to turn the family against me. He convinced his wife, my mother's sister, that I was a bad person and had wronged him. I don't think he told them about his plan to sell the business without my knowledge, but if he did, I'm sure he twisted the truth.

I believe Uncle Tony's intention in hiring my brother was to create a division within the family, knowing how close we were. Interestingly, for many years my mother asked me to bring my brother into the business. However, whenever I raised the issue to my uncle, it was rejected. After I left, and he hired my brother, he falsely told my mother that I had refused to bring him into the business. These actions caused a significant rift between my brother, me, and my parents. Unfortunately, my brother and I did not speak for many months.

The division in the family was difficult because we were all close. For example, even though my brothers Stephen and Mel were 6 and 8 years younger than me, we had a good relationship. Yes, there were brotherly arguments over the years, but we always made up.

Even though we had different birth mothers, we never referred to each other as half-brothers. We were and are brothers to this day. We were all raised in the same house as a family.

This was very evident when our father died in 2013. The night before the funeral, the priest came to the funeral home and asked to speak with my brothers and me about our father and his life. As the oldest, I told the priest stories about when my father met my mother, their courtship, etc. The priest was curious as to how I knew these things since I was speaking about witnessing the courtship. I explained to him that it was because my birth mother died, and I was around for my father's dates. The priest looked at my brothers and me and said,

"Oh, so you are half-brothers."

Almost in unison, and without even looking at each other, my brothers and I said to the priest,

"No, we are brothers; that's how we were raised." The priest was taken aback and was quite happy to hear our reaction.

Months after my brother was hired, the business couldn't survive, and the company closed, leading to my brother being let go. KPA closing was not what I hoped for when I left.

Ultimately, my family and I reconciled and moved past it, all of us realizing what was happening. We all regret the time we lost being angry with each other.

****

After news spread that I had left the company, I received calls from various people who were acquainted with my uncle and me. One memorable call was from my uncle's former accountant. She called to wish me luck and to share that she always anticipated this day would come. When I inquired why, she explained that during her monthly visits to my uncle's house to manage the books, she would observe my productivity and compensation and wonder,

"When do you think, Lenny is going to wake up?"

I asked her to clarify, and she explained that my compensation was based on how much my uncle needed to withdraw from the business for his family.

I was being paid based on what was left after he paid himself for his needs and business expenses instead of based on my revenue numbers. She cautioned them that this was very dangerous because one day, I would realize this and leave.

She told me that my uncle, aunt, and cousin all told her,

"Lenny won't do that. He doesn't have it in him."

They were betting on me continuing to be the subservient employee I was for all those years. That conversation convinced me that I had made the right decision to leave.

****

Regarding the organization of my business, I moved as quickly as possible to get myself up and running. I sublet a small office from a former colleague, set up the bank account, used my second mortgage money to fund it, and secured a phone number, business cards, and announcements.

In the first week of September, I was ready to start engaging in the market to attract new business. The month of August marked the longest period during which I was out of touch with clients and prospects. As we began sending out announcements to a newly built prospect list, several issues developed, which delayed my business launch.

First, I received a jury duty notice. I couldn't believe it! I tried to get a deferral, telling them I was starting a business. The court refused.

Then, I developed a debilitating pain in my back that traveled down my leg. The cause seemed to be the stress I was under. I had to see numerous doctors who prescribed muscle relaxers. These pills caused me to fall asleep at my home workstation. The pain was so bad that I had to walk with a cane and couldn't even travel to the city. Eventually, I was referred to a chiropractor who cured me. After serving several days of jury duty, I was able to start my launch again.

In mid-September, I again started reaching out to potential clients. Interestingly, when I told people I had left KPA and was starting my firm, their reactions were surprising. Each person I spoke with told me they didn't understand; they thought I owned KPA. I never made that claim to anyone while I represented my uncle's company; it was just assumed. My uncle primarily worked behind the scenes and did not interact directly with clients.

I started very slowly, almost as if I were starting from scratch. Every day, I would go to the office in the city, make calls, send emails, and try to drum up some business. Every night when I came home, my wife would ask me,

"Did anything happen today?"

When I sullenly told her that nothing happened, she would mark a big red X on that day's calendar. This continued for a few weeks. One evening, when I returned home, and she asked me again, I warned her that if she marked one more red X on the calendar, I would put that marker where the sun doesn't shine, although my words were a bit more colorful. She explained that she thought the visual Xs on the calendar would motivate me. She teased me to help me find the humor in the calendar with the red Xs.

I explained to her ....

A. I did not need motivation

B. I followed a business process that involved getting jobs, finding candidates, screening them, submitting them, scheduling interviews, and closing the deal. I was confident that something would happen but frustrated that it took longer than expected. I took on a few small temporary jobs that I could close and some full-time positions that we were in the process of filling. She understood my situation and promised to help by coming to the office a few days a week to assist with calls and resumes.

After about a month, a colleague from KPA I had hired a year and a half earlier, Franca Diona, called me. She told me she couldn't stay there any longer. Franca described my former employer as completely dysfunctional. She was miserable. Franca asked if she could come to work for me. We had worked together, so I knew of her talent and capabilities. However, I explained to her that as much as I would love to have her, I could not afford to hire anyone. She told me she believed in me and knew we would make money together.

"I will come for free," she said. "Just pay my carfare and lunch. Plus, I am leaving anyway; I can no longer stay here."

I reluctantly agreed, and since I was confident things would start happening soon, I told her that I would put her on a salary in about a month. She agreed and joined me shortly thereafter.

Franca, my wife, and I were in sync and determined to make progress.

By mid-November, there was a little activity but nothing earth-shattering. We received jobs to fill and scheduled interviews, but the process was relatively slow. I had a couple of temps on billing, and I even took on assignments writing marketing pieces for the career center of a local college—anything to generate some revenue.

Then, one day in November, we were in the office when I received a call from a client where we had some pending interviews. The client informed me that they were ready to offer a VP-level position to one of our candidates. That deal would generate a decent fee to my business. After I hung up, I couldn't contain my excitement. I screamed, hugged my wife, embraced Franca, and shared the news of the offer with them

"We are now on our way."

My wife understood my joy but didn't understand my comment.

"It is only one deal," she said.

"Yes," I told her. "That is right, but we have broken the logjam. This will be the first of many."

I felt it in my bones.

That deal allowed me to put Franca on a draw immediately, and we never looked back. We were in business. Franca has been with me since the beginning.

After we closed that deal, we started to develop some traction. I was aggressively reaching out to contacts to pitch my new business. Fortunately, as people began to hear about my latest venture, I started to get some referrals,

An old friend and contact referred me to one of his senior people in Europe who was starting a search for a senior banker for their NY office. I met this gentleman when he came to NY, and he awarded me the search. Energized, I began the search, giving it all I had.

Fortunately, I was successful in closing the deal. I also developed a good relationship with this European banker, who later brought me additional searches. Essentially, I returned to what I knew how to do... build the business, one client and one successful deal at a time.

One year later, I brought my daughter Heather in to assist us. Two years later, my son Matt joined us after graduating from college. My son Greg joined six years later when he finished school and was making a career change. Another former colleague, Dan McNichol, joined me shortly after that.

Several years after starting my business, I intentionally kept it relatively small and only hired people as needed. I admit that I had some successful hires and some not-so-successful. I guess it goes with the territory.

Chapter 23

"Feeding My Entrepreneurial Spirit"

After several years in business, my old friend and mentor, Angelo D'Avino, whom I spoke about earlier, approached me. He used to sublet space from my uncle. He subsequently left and leased his own space. He owned a recruiting firm (The ARD Group) that focused on the Insurance industry. He and his partner wanted to retire. He had a small team built around one solid producer, Scott Cohen. I asked him why he didn't just sell it to Scott. He explained that Scott was a great producer but needed someone like me with a business aptitude to help him. At first, I turned him down, not wanting to distract from my business. Angelo was persistent and asked me to reconsider.

I asked him if Scott knew of his plans. He said not yet. Recollecting what I had gone through with my uncle, I made an offer to Angelo.

"I will do this on two conditions. One, Scott must immediately be made aware of your plan, and two, he must become my partner in the business. I will not do to him what was done to me. "

Angelo appreciated my position and agreed to schedule a meeting with Scott and me. I knew Scott, and I knew his strengths and weaknesses.

We did become partners, buying out Angelo and his partner; Scott was a great partner and friend to me and a fantastic producer. Our skills complemented each other. We ran that business from 2008 until 2020.

Scott's untimely death from COVID-19 in April of 2020 ended that partnership. It was a devasting loss for me, personally and professionally. I closed the business and folded it into my company.

I did try some other ventures; some were successful, others weren't. That's business!

****

Fortunately, my company had generally low turnover until COVID-19 hit in 2020. That along with my cancer diagnosis, which I successfully survived, were nothing more than distractions.

Those setbacks have not deterred us from being optimistic about our continued success. Resilience is my middle name.

Chapter 24

Over Two Decades and Growing!

The last twenty-plus years of running my business have brought challenges and triumphs.

Even though I ran my uncle's business as if it were my own, there were aspects I didn't know. I no longer had anyone to turn to when making decisions. All decisions are mine, right or wrong. I needed to be confident that my instincts were and are correct.

While I'm certain I've made mistakes over the past years of managing my own company, I'm also confident that most of my decisions were correct.

253

I've learned that it's crucial to be adaptable in business, to pivot when necessary, and to be open to new ways of doing things.

My strategy for success in the recruitment and search industry is to look at opportunities and prospects that other firms ignore. I focus on building relationships that will lead to business and referrals. I take a long-term approach to the business and position ourselves as 'problem solvers,' not just recruiters.

While the industry has certainly changed since my days 50 years ago, the basic tenets of the business have remained the same.

Our methodology and approach remain steadfast regardless of economic fluctuations. Although there may be busy and slower periods, I firmly believe in consistently working hard. I have

254

personally adhered to this principle and instilled it in my team and children. Maintaining a consistent pace yields results. There will always be a company needing employees and candidates open to making a move, irrespective of the state of the economy. Today, we have access to more tools and automation, and the key is to use them wisely.

****

Having brought my sons and daughter into the company, I could probably write another book about these past twenty years. It has been an exciting journey.

Given the time that has passed since I left my uncle, I've come to realize that age brings wisdom. I understand some of the decisions he made, although I can't say I entirely agree with them. All I would have liked was a bit more transparency. I am grateful for the education and career opportunity he provided me. However, I wish he had treated me more like an adult and recognized my contribution to his success. I understand that there may have been other influences that led him to treat me as he did. As for his plan to sell the business, I felt hurt, betrayed, and angry. I was hurt that he didn't feel he could trust me with a decision that would benefit his family, and I felt betrayed that he was reneging on specific promises he made to me.

I was angry that he treated me like a piece of office furniture that could be sold without discussion. He didn't even allow me to help vet the buyer that he was handing my career and the future of my family over to.

I often wonder if his motivation was greed, fear, a sense of mortality, or the overprotectiveness of his family. Or all of the above. I remembered what he preached to me all the years I was with him, the biblical phrase: "Don't let your right hand know what your left hand is doing." He truly believed that, so he kept me in the dark about his plans. My perspective on that adage is that information should be freely shared with people whom you trust. I don't believe every aspect of one's life must be an open book. It's important to carefully assess each situation to determine what information is crucial to share and with whom.

The situation could have been handled differently. I don't know if either of us would have had a different outcome. Hindsight is not always 20/20. He passed away in 2013, one week before my father. Unfortunately, his son had passed away several years prior. I did not speak with either of them after 2002 when I left.

****

A year and a month after starting ACG, my wife, family, and I moved into a newly constructed house. It has been a positive change, and my business has not just survived but thrived. I have been passionate about this business since I started at 15. Assisting companies with their hiring needs, solving problems, and helping people with their careers is truly gratifying. Over the past 20-plus years, I have been fortunate to provide for my family in ways I never imagined. Building a great team and staying true to my beliefs in operating a business and treating employees, clients, and candidates has been a key part of my success.

As I age, I don't foresee myself retiring anytime soon. I enjoy the business challenges and being present to counsel and guide my team and my family.

258

I've never been solely motivated by money. Money has always been a means to an end that fuels the business. I've always prioritized the quality of service over monetary gain. I encourage my team to approach all deals with the same level of effort, regardless of the amount of money involved. The focus is on providing exceptional service that strengthens the brand. My journey has shown that financial success naturally follows by operating in this manner. Money is essential for the business and the livelihood of everyone involved, but it shouldn't be the sole motivator. Doing a good job is what drives us. I hope this business will outlive me and thrive for generations.

Reflecting on my career and my life, I recall the words of the song made famous by Frank Sinatra and Paul Anka: "Regrets, I've had a few, but then again, too few to mention. I did what I had to do and saw it through without exemption. I did it my way.

Chapter 25

Len Rules For Success in Life and Business

I have lived my life following specific beliefs that have served me well. I am happy to share them

- Honor Your Commitments: If you commit to something, follow through.
- Be Punctual: Arrive 15 minutes early. Being on time is being late.
- Show Respect: Treat everyone with respect, regardless of their title.
- Work Hard: Put in more effort than others.
- Surround Yourself with Smart People: You don't need to be the smartest—being around smart people makes you look smarter.

- Build Relationships: Develop connections with clients, candidates, and vendors. Relationships may take years to yield results; focus on the long-term.
- Prioritize Family: Family is everything. Take care of them.
- Be Nice to the people you meet on the way up; they are the same ones you will meet on the way down It's just as easy to be kind as it is to be nasty.
- Influence Wisely: Your business actions affect people's lives. Choose your impact carefully.
- Be Honest: Be truthful with yourself and others. Avoid self-deception.
- Live Within Your Means: Avoid unnecessary debt. If you have debt, repay it.
- Be Authentic: No need to impress anyone. Be genuine.
- Find Joy in Your livelihood: Do what you love, and it won't feel like work.
- Engage Personally: Pick up the phone, meet for coffee, or have meals. Don't rely solely on email and text.
- Be Inquisitive: People enjoy talking about themselves. Encourage them to share.

- Make Connections: Introduce people to each other. They'll remember you as the connector.
- Success is a journey: Focus on the process, not just the end goal.
- Use a To-Do List: Write things down to stay organized and accomplish tasks.
- Plan Ahead: A daily plan helps you achieve your goals.
- Dress Appropriately: It's better to be overdressed than underdressed; you can always adjust.
- Be Memorable: Make a lasting impression.
- Value Problem-Solving Over Money: Focus on solving problems; financial rewards will follow.
- Do the Right Thing: Always act with integrity.
- Be Present: Showing up is half the battle; being fully engaged is the other half.
- Cherish Friendships: Value and maintain your friendships.
- Respond Promptly: Return every call, email, and text to show you care and are attentive.
- Be Genuine: Ensure your interactions are sincere.

- You are NEVER too old to learn something new: Never feel you know it all. BE open to continue learning
- Help with Passion: If you commit to solving a problem or filling a role, do so passionately. If you can't, don't commit.
- Learn from Mistakes: If someone takes advantage of you once, it's a mistake; if it happens again, it's your fault for allowing it